Fundamentals of Library Supervision

ALA FUNDAMENTALS SERIES

FUNDAMENTALS OF ELECTRONIC RESOURCES MANAGEMENT
by Alana Verminski and Kelly Marie Blanchat

FUNDAMENTALS OF TECHNICAL SERVICES
by John Sandstrom and Liz Miller

FUNDAMENTALS FOR THE ACADEMIC LIAISON
by Richard Moniz, Jo Henry, and Joe Eshleman

FUNDAMENTALS OF CHILDREN'S SERVICES, 2ND ED.
by Michael Sullivan

FUNDAMENTALS OF LIBRARY INSTRUCTION
by Monty L. McAdoo

FUNDAMENTALS OF LIBRARY SUPERVISION, 3RD ED.
by Beth McNeil

FUNDAMENTALS OF MANAGING REFERENCE COLLECTIONS
by Carol A. Singer

FUNDAMENTALS OF REFERENCE
by Carolyn M. Mulac

FUNDAMENTALS OF TECHNICAL SERVICES MANAGEMENT
by Sheila S. Intner, with Peggy Johnson

SMALL PUBLIC LIBRARY MANAGEMENT
by Jane Pearlmutter and Paul Nelson

ALA FUNDAMENTALS SERIES

Fundamentals of Library Supervision

THIRD EDITION

Beth McNeil

An imprint of the American Library Association

Chicago   2017

BETH McNEIL is professor and dean of the library at Iowa State University. Prior to joining Iowa State in 2015, McNeil served in associate dean roles at Purdue University and at the University of Nebraska–Lincoln. She received a PhD in human sciences with a leadership focus from the University of Nebraska–Lincoln and an MS degree in library and information science and an AB degree in English from the University of Illinois at Urbana-Champaign. Her publications include previous editions of *Library Supervision, Patron Behavior in Libraries* (1996), and *Human Resource Management in Today's Academic Library* (2004).

© 2017 by the American Library Association

Extensive effort has gone into ensuring the reliability of the information in this book; however, the publisher makes no warranty, express or implied, with respect to the material contained herein.

ISBNs
978-0-8389-1554-7 (paper)
978-0-8389-1570-7 (PDF)
978-0-8389-1571-4 (ePub)
978-0-8389-1572-1 (Kindle)

Library of Congress Cataloging-in-Publication Data

Names: McNeil, Beth. | Giesecke, Joan. Fundamentals of library supervision.
Title: Fundamentals of library supervision / Beth McNeil.
Description: Third edition. | Chicago : Neal-Schuman, an imprint of the American Library Association, 2017. | Series: ALA fundamentals series | Previous edition authored by Joan Giesecke and Beth McNeil. | Includes bibliographical references and index.
Identifiers: LCCN 2017002509| ISBN 9780838915547 (pbk. : alk. paper) | ISBN 9780838915707 (pdf) | ISBN 9780838915714 (epub) | ISBN 9780838915721 (kindle)
Subjects: LCSH: Library personnel management—United States. | Supervision of employees.
Classification: LCC Z682.2.U5 G54 2017 | DDC 023/.9—dc23 LC record available at https://lccn.loc.gov/2017002509

Cover Alejandra Diaz. Image © Julie/Adobe Stock. Text composition in the Melior and Din typefaces by Dianne M. Rooney.

⊗ This paper meets the requirements of ANSI/NISO Z39.48-1992 (Permanence of Paper).

Printed in the United States of America

21 20 19 18 17   5 4 3 2 1

ALA Neal-Schuman purchases fund advocacy, awareness, and accreditation programs for library professionals worldwide.

Contents

Figures

Preface

Do you enjoy bringing people together and helping them to do their best? If you do, then you are ready to think about supervision and management.

Today's managers, supervisors, team leaders, project managers, unit heads, and organization leaders face a more complex and rapidly changing environment. Roles vary. Depending on one's position and the organization, in just one day, an individual may need to lead, manage, and supervise, and all before noon. All three are roles that today's supervisors need to play, and the setting changes constantly. Today's workplace and workforce are different from those of even just a few years ago. Managers may find themselves overseeing four to five generations of staff, each with its own characteristics and needs. Each individual and each group may respond best to a specific supervisor's or manager's different style.

The legal environment is also more complex, with laws addressing discrimination, sexual harassment, health issues, accommodation requirements, restroom facilities, and other personnel issues. Today's supervisor needs to keep up with legal changes and evolving cultural norms if he or she is to lead in a culturally competent organization, not to mention avoid legal challenges.

Supervisors must take a leadership role in providing support for their staff and ensuring the library can meet its goals and objectives. Poor supervisory skills will only compound the morale problems that arise during difficult times. Excellent supervisory skills can lead to departments and units that not only cope with the challenges they face but also are able to move forward and become excellent organizations.

While our world is more complicated, it is also more exciting. Managers have more flexibility in how they structure their units or organizations. They have more options for delegating tasks, establishing goals, and encouraging staff development. They can build high-powered teams that surpass traditionally structured units.

This book attempts to cover the fundamentals of good supervision and management and to bring together practical advice with basic commonsense approaches to solving today's management challenges. Whether you are just getting started as a new supervisor or are already an experienced manager, I hope you will find that the topics covered here provide you with an overview and foundation for many of the tasks and responsibilities of being a supervisor, manager, and leader in your organization. Practical skills covered include hiring, interviewing, orienting, and appraising employees; managing rewards; budget basics; planning and organizing work; facilities, space, and safety; project management; and conducting meetings. Areas necessary for solid leadership—from communication skills to organizational climate, motivation, and diversity and inclusion—are also included.

Throughout the book, examples of supervisory opportunities and challenges are portrayed through the experiences of two new supervisors, Chris and Jamie. Chris is a manager who was hired from outside the organization after a national search. Jamie is a manager who was promoted from within the organization. Their similar challenges and different perspectives will help illustrate ways that supervisors can address the various tasks and challenges their jobs entail. The examples and stories in this book are composites created from a variety of experiences and organizations. All names, circumstances, and details have been altered. Any resemblance to real people, though possible, is coincidental.

As a supervisor and manager, you will have on-the-job opportunities to learn about and practice many of the common attributes of leadership, including the following:

- Flexibility, adaptability, and a willingness to accept and manage change
- Visionary, strategic planning and resource management
- Cultural competence
- Setting priorities, managing time, and multitasking
- Advocacy
- Innovation and collaboration

- Self-awareness, self-knowledge, and emotional intelligence
- Decision making and problem solving
- Understanding of library trends
- Influence[1]

When you excel at supervision and management and become adept at these skills and attributes, you will be a leader in your organization. Best wishes and enjoy!

NOTE

1. Shorette Ammons-Stephens, Holly J. Cole, Catherine Fraser Riehle, and William H. Weare, "Developing Core Leadership Competencies for the Library Profession," *Library Leadership and Management* 23, no. 2 (2009): 63–74; Peter Hernon, Ronald R. Powell, and Arthur P. Young, "University Library Directors in the Association of Research Libraries: The Next Generation, Part One," *College and Research Libraries*, 62, no. 2 (2001): 116–46.

Supervising Individuals

1

Today's Workplace

Today's workplace is significantly different from the one that existed even a few years ago. Change is a way of life. Organizations face new competition, changing technology, mergers and acquisitions, bankruptcies, changing consumer expectations, and economic instability in the normal course of events. We work in a global environment, with potential suppliers and customers located anywhere. Jobs are outsourced. Multinational companies are learning how to blend cultures and develop management structures that can be successful in multiple environments. Technological changes impact all aspects of business, from financial systems to human resources and knowledge-base systems. Furthermore, managers face the instability that can result from mergers and acquisitions as well as from the blending of different types of organizations within the same industry. Managing becomes more challenging when you are not sure if the top management of the company is arranging a restructuring or planning to sell the company to another owner. Long-range plans quickly become short-range strategies for survival if you do not think you have a long time frame to protect your own career. To compound this uncertainty, today's managers also face an uncertain economic environment, with budget reductions, downsizing, and restructuring of financial plans having become facts of life. Externally, organizations face the challenge of new expectations from customers who seek to customize anything they can, including restaurant meals, and want everything quickly. Satisfying customer demands when those demands are always changing compounds the challenges of planning and organizing work for effectiveness and efficiency. The changing political landscape also makes planning more challenging. With the 2008 election of Barack Obama, the first African American president, came changes to federal regulations on information infrastructure and policies around open research and data. Donald Trump's election and the new Republican administration's directives to federal agencies during its first month in office signal significant changes to the communication practices of these taxpayer-supported agencies. Librarians must be familiar with the national, state, and local environments to assess the impact of any changes on their libraries and larger organizations.

Trends

Libraries are not immune to these different forces, and library managers need to understand how these forces and other trends impact their organizations.

Competition. Libraries face competition from a variety of sources. Today's students, citizens, or company employees are more likely to try search engines—Google, for example—first for information than they are to check with a librarian. People of all ages can also be found studying in bookstores with cafés and comfortable seating rather than in libraries. Understanding the context in which the library is situated is crucial. Managers and other leaders must tie library initiatives to the larger organization's strategic plan for vision and mission. Library managers need to understand this world of competition if they are to position their libraries to remain a vital part of their communities or organizations.

With competition comes the importance of promoting collections and services. No longer can libraries afford to sit back and assume that everyone knows what libraries can contribute to the community. Instead, librarians must develop plans to explain why libraries are still needed and how they play a vital role in the information-rich world we live in. The American Library Association's @your library, Libraries Transform, and Expert in the Library campaigns are some of the ways libraries can market their services and advocate for and advertise their worth. As libraries face budget reductions, librarians need to actively engage with their communities, solicit library user support, and demonstrate how libraries can contribute to the economic and social well-being of their communities or campuses in order to stay relevant.

Technology. Rapidly changing technology is a way of life in today's libraries. The library manager who waits to find the perfect system before implementing new technologies will not be successful. Librarians have to become risk takers, trying new technologies even though the results are not guaranteed. Moreover, managers must let go of the idea that once a decision on technology has been made and hardware and software have been purchased, they can keep that technology for a long time. Hardware and software change regularly, and librarians must find ways to stay current if libraries are to remain vital to their patrons. Finding funds to upgrade workstations on a three-year cycle, for example, will change how budgets are structured and how priorities are set.

Mobile technology has changed how people communicate. In 2011, one-third of Americans owned a smartphone; today, nearly two-thirds do. In the young adult group, this figure is close 85 percent.[1] Information is available anytime, anywhere, and it is easily accessible from phones, watches, tablets, and other mobile devices. Libraries appear as physical spaces, websites, RSS feeds, blogs, Facebook pages, or part of the search toolbar. When library users e-mail or IM (instant message) a question, they could be anywhere—on the other side of the world or just across the room. These changes alter how librarians think about services and service delivery.

Technology changes also impact internal organizational structures. With networked resources and online systems available in many libraries, managers may find that their staffs include employees who want to telecommute rather than work on-site. Supervising these employees takes careful planning and creativity to ensure that productivity measures are met and that these staff members feel a part of the overall unit or department. The use of technology also brings ergonomic concerns to the workplace, with supervisors needing to address issues of safe workplaces and workstation arrangements that will decrease the chances of employees developing health problems, such as carpal tunnel syndrome. While previously any table or chair might do, today's workers who spend all day working at computers need a work space that can be adjusted to meet their individual needs. Furthermore, ubiquitous network options and handheld devices mean that employees can be connected at any time to their workplace and their e-mail, no matter where they may be located physically. Work time can expand to include any time of the day or night. Supervisors and managers now need to address the issue of staff who may work too many hours, complicating the discussion of what constitutes work and work-related activities.

Technology also impacts how decisions can be made. Supervisors may now have access to a variety of data on workload, productivity, and customer satisfaction not available previously. They can use computer systems to monitor productivity measures, such as how long it takes to catalog or process items or to download records and add metadata, and to gauge how long someone takes to answer a question on a chat reference service as well as the accuracy of the answer. Data can make decision making more transparent, but it also can be used to obscure how decisions are actually made.

Mergers and acquisitions. Changes in organizational structures are occurring as public and school libraries are being blended in the same space, corporations are centralizing information services by eliminating smaller local collections and services, and academic libraries are closing branches and building virtual libraries instead of physical collections in order to serve dispersed populations. These types of changes have occurred at various times in the history of libraries, but today, with the ever-changing information world, managers may face situations that they never thought would impact their institutions.

Customer expectations. Customers want access to a wide variety of information resources and services at times and from locations and on devices that are convenient for them. Libraries that are not customer focused will not be supported and sustainability will become an issue.

Economic uncertainty. Libraries are all too familiar with the problems of budget and staffing reductions. In tough economic times, libraries may be seen as less central to the core mission of an organization, less central to the core activities of a school, and less important to a state, county, or city that must fund mandated initiatives and social programs. For example, in a survey of citizens in Lincoln, Nebraska, on their perceptions of city services, citizens rated libraries as essential services. Nonetheless, when asked to prioritize the funding of city services, citizens rated fire and police as essential and libraries as nice but not crucial for the city.[2] To remain essential, librarians must find ways to demonstrate how services and collections impact the success of their cities, universities, and other institutions.

Changing workforce. Perhaps the most noticeable trend is the changing demographics of the United States. The population is becoming increasingly diverse. Supervisors need to learn to recruit and retain staff from a variety of ethnic and racial backgrounds. Another demographic change is the number of generations in the workplace, with five generations of workers now a part of many of our institutions. Supervisors cannot assume that all employees will behave and react to the organizational environment in the same way. Supervisors must consider how to build relationships and partnerships with staff to get the work done, rather than thinking they can simply give orders and have staff carry out those orders.

Global economy. While it may be easy to think of one's library as a local institution, libraries are very much connected to and influenced by the global economy. The regular news of mergers in the publishing field means libraries are buying many of their reference and scholarly resources from companies headquartered in Europe and other countries. Acquisition budget planning has to include the impact of exchange rates as well as the impact of inflation.

Libraries and publishers are also taking advantage of the global economy by outsourcing digitization work to countries such as China and India, where labor costs are less than in the United States. Partnerships are being created, too, as US libraries join with libraries in other countries to provide online real-time assistance on a twenty-four-hour basis. These partnerships are helping libraries expand services to meet the demand for service in our 24/7 world.

Today's library managers and supervisors need to be aware of these trends and try to plan for how they will impact their own institutions and organizations. They must understand the big picture of the information field if they are to be successful in an environment of change.

Changing Roles of Managers and Supervisors

Not only are the organizations we work in changing, but the role of the supervisor is also changing. In the middle of the twentieth century, the manager's role could be described by the acronym POSDCoRB: Planning, Organizing, Staffing, Directing, Coordinating, Reporting, and Budgeting. (See figure 1.1 for a description of the manager's role in the twentieth century.) While these roles still exist in our organizations, it is more likely in today's environment that these activities are shared between the supervisors and the staff. A supervisor is more coach than director and more facilitator than commander. New roles for supervisors include recognizing and recruiting talent, teaching staff new skills and promoting learning, understanding the organization's culture, and understanding organizational power.

Recruiting talent. Successful supervisors are learning new ways to recruit. They are learning that they need to recruit talent and ability rather than looking only at skills. Supervisors know they can teach skills to talented

FIGURE 1.1
POSDCoRB: Supervisory Roles in the Twentieth Century

ROLE	RESPONSIBILITIES
Planning	Managers were responsible for determining organizational goals and deciding how the organization should meet those goals.
Organizing	Managers determined how the work would be divided among organizational units and decided what procedures would be used to accomplish those tasks.
Staffing	Managers were responsible for the personnel decisions in their units, including hiring and evaluating staff.
Directing	Managers directed the work of others, deciding who would complete which tasks.
Coordinating	Managers coordinated activities between units. Staff were responsible only for work within their own units.
Reporting	Managers were responsible for reporting on unit accomplishments and keeping upper management informed about unit progress.
Budgeting	Managers were responsible for the unit's budget, determining how resources would be divided and monitoring to make sure that budgets were met.

employees easier than they can teach someone to be talented. Without the key talents and abilities needed to do a job, a staff member is unlikely to excel. In today's market, where recruiting is very competitive, it is important to recruit the best staff possible so the unit can succeed and grow.

Promoting learning. Staff today want a job that provides personal satisfaction, one where they can control their own destinies and where they have a voice in what happens.[3] In organizations that promote learning and encourage staff development, staff are more likely to find the satisfaction they seek. Supervisors who promote a partnership approach to the management of the unit are more likely to create an environment where staff have input in the unit and feel appreciated for their efforts.

Organizational culture. Successful supervisors understand the organizational culture in which they operate. Supervisors need to know how the organization measures success, how rewards are determined, how mistakes are handled, how decisions are made, and how risk is tolerated. They also understand the time frame in which the organization operates. For example, some libraries work on a semester system, some on the school year, and some on the fiscal year. These time frames impact how objectives are measured and how the pace of the work is likely to be set.

Supervisors can learn their organization's culture by carefully listening to others, observing how things are done, keeping an open mind about workflow and processes, observing who succeeds and why, and remembering to look at the big picture beyond their own units. Setting aside time to reflect on organizational activities and keeping notes on what works and what does not work will help identify the key elements in the culture.

Organizational power. Power is a natural part of an organization. New supervisors should study the organizational chart to see how their units fit into the overall structure and with each other, and then they should periodically review their units' work within the overall organizational structure. It also helps to identify what activities are not reflected on the organizational chart and then learn how these functions are dispersed in the organization. Understanding relationships will also help in identifying organizational politics. It helps, for example, to know how colleagues are connected and the history of relationships. Questions to consider and possibly ask of a trusted colleague might include these: Do they belong to the same groups? Do these people form an alliance in the organization? How does the distribution of power in the organization relate to the political relationships? Thinking explicitly about the organization and reflecting upon what goes on will give supervisors a better chance of developing successful ways to work that will be rewarded.

Changing Competencies

With these new roles and responsibilities, managers and supervisors need to develop a variety of competencies beyond technical expertise to succeed in their jobs. Skills of human resources management, team building, and leadership are the foundation of successful management at all levels of the organization. To be a good leader, one must be a good supervisor and manager.[4] Plan on putting the following competencies to work daily as you develop your skills as a manager:

Interpersonal skills. Supervision is about creating relationships. Good interpersonal skills, also known as people skills, are a must.

Communication skills. Become an effective communicator. Written, verbal, and active-listening communication skills are crucial. Recognize both the value of and the pitfalls for online communication.

Problem solving and decision making. Learning to analyze data and using that data to resolve problems will help you work effectively. Using good judgment is also a key success factor.

Initiative. Taking the initiative, anticipating needs, and taking action are signs of a good supervisor. Finding the balance between listening and speed of action is an important leadership skill.

Delegation. Learning to appropriately delegate the right tasks to the right people is a skill that is often overlooked. Take time to learn how to delegate effectively and practice that skill.

Time management. Managing your own time as well as the time of your staff will make your unit more successful and able to complete assigned projects and tasks. Social media can be a powerful marketing and communication tool as well as a major time sink.

Meetings management. Much of the work in today's organizations is done through groups and teams. Knowing how to run an efficient and effective meeting will make your groups more successful.

Ensuring that meetings are not seen as an alternative to work and as a waste of time and effort is an important skill.

Customer service. Know the needs of your patrons, your internal customers, and your external constituencies, and be sure everyone in your unit is focused on how they can meet those needs. Service is everyone's business.[5]

Leadership Skills

Leadership skills are no longer solely the purview of upper management. Today, all librarians need to understand, practice, and demonstrate good leadership skills regardless of their formal roles in their libraries. These skills or strategies help when leading committees in their libraries, communities, or professional associations and enable managers to keep up with change as they prepare their employees for new roles and new challenges. Many books describe what is needed for successful leadership. Max De Pree, in his book *Leadership Is an Art*, about Herman Miller, Inc., notes three leadership themes as essential to artful leadership: integrity, knack for relationships, and community building.[6] In the book *Creating Magic: 10 Common Sense Leadership Strategies from a Life at Disney*, Lee Cockerell describes the ten leadership strategies that the Disney corporation found to be most effective.[7] These strategies, discussed in the remainder of this section, are particularly applicable to service industries, such as libraries, where customer or patron satisfaction is a key success factor.

STRATEGY ONE

Value Your Employees

As a supervisor, you want to develop an inclusive style that values every employee in your unit and in your organization. Cockerell uses the acronym RAVE to describe this strategy: respect, appreciate, and value everyone.[8] In *The New One Minute Manager*, Ken Blanchard and Spencer Johnson refer to this as "catch them doing something right."[9] Be sure you sincerely thank staff for a job well done. Staff will know if you are only going through the motions of being sincere and will resent your efforts.

Look for Creative Change Strategies

As a supervisor, you want to keep asking how you can improve on processes and structure. How can you make the unit a better, more effective one? What types of creative changes will bring the best results? By being open to new ideas you will be more likely to see possible changes that will bring positive results.

Hire the Best

Perhaps the most important decisions you make as a manager or a supervisor are hiring decisions because your staff become the embodiment of your library brand. Customers will judge your area by the response they get from your staff. Always hire the best talent you can. As noted in *First, Break All the Rules*, hire talent and train for skills.[10] You can teach someone new skills, but you cannot teach them to be talented. When you have good people working for you, your unit will be successful. If you have to spend most of your time correcting hiring errors, your unit will not excel.

Training Is Key

Providing regular and ongoing training for your unit is essential. If your institution has a staff development program, be sure your staff are taking advantage of training opportunities. If your organization does not provide this type of support, look for training opportunities you can bring to your unit and talk to colleagues about implementing a staff development program. Is there a webinar available on a particular process or challenge your unit is facing? Is there someone in your community who can help with skill building? Be creative as you look for opportunities to coach your staff to excel.

Eliminate Hassles

Look for ways that you can make processes and procedures more streamlined and effective for your patrons and your staff. Try being a customer in your own library. Can you easily fill out an online form for a service? Can you find the information you need to answer a reference question? You may also want to borrow ideas from other service organizations. Have you experienced great service? What made the experience so successful? Are there elements of the service that you can bring to your unit?

STRATEGY SIX

Learn the Truth, Then Act

In the 1970s, management literature referred to "management by walking around." This style is still effective in many organizations and should include being connected to the virtual environment, both with library users and with staff. Know what is going on in your unit. When someone brings you a problem, listen carefully and get the whole story. Verify facts before you act so that you are sure you are working with the best information possible before you determine how to resolve an issue. You will be in a better position to assess information when you have a thorough and current understanding of the activities in your unit.

STRATEGY SEVEN

Reward the Behaviors You Want to See

Reward the behaviors you want and do not encourage the behaviors that should be eliminated. Too often, supervisors either ignore poor performance or spend so much time trying to correct a problem that they forget to reward and encourage those who are performing well. Do not take your best employees for granted. Instead, recognize and encourage excellence. And be creative about recognition. You will find that you get the behaviors you reward.

STRATEGY EIGHT

Keep Learning

In a world of change, supervisors and managers need to keep an open mind and seek new ideas and innovations if they are to be successful. You need to stay current on trends, learn what others in the field are doing to meet the challenges of the day, and seek to implement best practices. As Cockerell notes, "it is the learners who inherit the future. The learned . . . live in a world that no longer exists."[11] To avoid trying to manage the past, become an active learner.

STRATEGY NINE

Always Be Professional, in Person and Online

In this day and age, that one picture of you with a lamp shade on your head is likely to appear on the Internet. A sarcastic remark on your Facebook page or Twitter feed could be shared with all your colleagues. As a professional, you will want to be sure you project an appropriate image and model the qualities you value. When you treat your staff with respect and value their expertise, you will have a strong, well-functioning unit that will excel.

STRATEGY TEN

Be An Ethical Manager

Leading with integrity is important if you want your staff to commit to the unit and to support you. You are also responsible for demonstrating positive values to your unit and creating a culture of inclusiveness.

Summary

Change is simply a way of life for the field of library and information science. While the core functions of libraries—providing access to an organized collection of materials and providing assistance in using those materials—remain the same, how libraries fulfill those functions has changed and will continue to change at faster and faster speeds. Technological advances make it possible for libraries to provide access to a wide range and different types of materials that no single library owns. Libraries can serve customers from around the world as easily as they serve the people who walk into their buildings. The library is truly a global enterprise.

In such a world, managers in today's libraries must embrace change. The management strategies that worked many years ago are not successful in today's volatile environment. For success, managers and supervisors need to stay aware of the many trends that impact the field of library and information science and learn how to bring the best of these changes into their units and organizations.

NOTES

1. Andrew Sullivan, "I Used to Be a Human Being," *New York* (September 19, 2016), 35.
2. University of Nebraska Public Policy Center, "Priority Lincoln: Budgeting for Outcomes" (Final report, May 29, 2008), 32, http://ppc.unl.edu/wp-content/uploads/2008/05/PriorityLincolnFinalReport.pdf.
3. Gary McClain and Deborah S. Romaine, *The Everything Managing People Book* (Avon, MA: Adams Media, 2002), 11.
4. Cliff Goodwin, *Supervisor's Survival Guide*, 10th ed. (Upper Saddle River, NJ: Pearson Education, 2006), 38.
5. William A. Salmon, *The New Supervisor's Survival Manual* (New York: AMACOM, 1999), 5–7.
6. Max De Pree, *Leadership Is an Art* (New York: Crown Business, 2004), ix–xi.
7. Lee Cockerell, *Creating Magic: 10 Common Sense Leadership Strategies from a Life at Disney* (New York: Doubleday, 2008), 54–55.
8. Ibid.
9. Ken Blanchard and Spencer Johnson, *The New One Minute Manager* (New York: HarperCollins, 2015), 49.
10. Marcus Buckingham and Curt Coffman, *First, Break All the Rules: What the World's Greatest Managers Do Differently* (New York: Simon and Schuster, 1999), 67.
11. Cockerell, *Creating Magic*, 208.

2

Hiring and Interviewing

Chris has just been given the task of heading a new three-person team in the university library to develop a research data service for the campus community. Chris is fortunate to be able to hire two librarians to work on the data team. Chris would like to call up a few friends from library school to work with her on this project, but she knows she cannot do that. First, Chris's organization requires that she do a national or regional search to find the best people for the job. Secondly, even though Chris knows some librarians who have skills with data, she is familiar with research that shows diverse groups are more productive and do the best work with more creative results.[1] Chris has never conducted a search before. What should she do? Chris asks the human resources staff for help.

Determining the work that needs to be accomplished, selecting employees to do that work, and deciding how to measure success for the program are some of the most important responsibilities of a supervisory position. Whether you are filling an existing vacancy or are fortunate to have an entirely new position, consider carefully what sort of work needs to be accomplished. Your library or larger organization very likely has guidelines for writing job descriptions, advertising positions, interviewing applicants, and making hiring decisions. Working within these guidelines, you will be able to interview and hire the best candidates for your open positions.

Job Descriptions

The hiring process begins with a good position description. Job descriptions include the basic functions of the position and serve a variety of purposes. For supervisors, the position description provides a framework for staff performance evaluations. For the employee, the position description identifies the essential job functions and helps the employee to understand what is expected of him or her. For an organization's human resources office, a position description provides a basis for understanding the role and includes content important to advertising the position.

Job descriptions should include a job summary, a detailed list of duties and responsibilities, necessary qualifications and skills, and, if pertinent, any physical requirements for the position. The listing of duties and responsibilities should be detailed enough that a new employee can understand what tasks must be accomplished. Many position descriptions include the percentage of time devoted to each task as well as an indication of whether the task is essential to the position. The use of clear, concise, and consistent language is very important for delineating duties and responsibilities, particularly when a task may be done by more than one employee.[2]

For Chris, developing job descriptions for her new positions is a challenge. Still, she needs to outline the key tasks of the job and the qualifications that are needed. For these data positions, Chris might ask for experience with data and metadata and an understanding of or experience with the federal agency guidelines. Because these are entry-level positions, Chris may put experience under "preferred qualifications" and seek people with a strong interest in data management and demonstrated solid interpersonal skills.

Hiring Processes

Libraries, like all employers, have requirements and guidelines for hiring related to federal employment and equal opportunity legislation. If you work in a large library, you may have a human resources person in the library. For some public libraries, the city government's human resources office may be the source for guidelines and regulations. For small college or university libraries, a central campus human resources office may handle personnel for all of the campus. Depending on the situation in your library, always work with the appropriate human resources department to be sure that you are following all the necessary procedures.

Preparing for the Interview

Prior to interviewing a candidate, review the requirements of the job. Review the position description (which lists the specific tasks to be performed on the job as well as the methods, techniques, technology, and tools or equipment used to accomplish these tasks). Make note of unusual working conditions and other specific demands of the job in order to adapt the interview to elicit relevant information.

Develop your interview questions well in advance and relate those questions to the requirements of the job. Even experienced supervisors may occasionally wonder about the appropriateness of asking particular questions. The best advice to follow is that if a question is not job related, do not ask it. Questions about an applicant's name, address, age, race/color/national origin, gender, religion/creed, sexual orientation, citizenship, marital/parental/family status, military service, criminal record, or disability should not be asked unless they pertain to the job. For example, if you need to verify degree or past employment information, it is all right to ask whether an applicant's work records are under another name, for the purpose of accessing these records. However, you should not ask the ethnic origin of a name, inquire whether a woman is a Miss, Mrs., or Ms., or request a maiden name. Because diversity is such an important issue in today's libraries, and we want to convey this to our job applicants, it may be tempting to ask questions related to a candidate's ethnicity during interviews. It is permissible to state that your library is an equal opportunity employer. However, you should not ask anything that would require a candidate to indicate race, color, national origin,

FIGURE 2.1

Legal and Illegal Questions: A Quiz

QUESTION	ANSWER
You are interviewing a woman for a position in your circulation department. She mentioned during the interview that she is a single parent. The position requires a weekend shift once each month. Is it okay to ask, "Can you arrange for child care?"	NO. Even though she volunteered the information about having children, this question is not appropriate. However, you can ask if she is willing to work the required schedule.
You are interviewing a man for a position in your access services department. The position is responsible for collecting money from photocopy machines. Is it permissible to ask him, "Have you ever been arrested?"	NO. However, it is okay to ask him if he has ever been convicted of theft because the crime is related to the position. Convictions, if related to the position, are pertinent. Arrests, however, are not.
You want to hire a metadata librarian to work with a unique digital collection of materials from South America. You would like to know what languages the applicant can read and at what level. Is it permissible to ask a question such as, "What languages do you read fluently?"	YES. This question is perfectly acceptable because the answer is relevant to the performance of the job.

or gender. For additional examples of legal and illegal questions, see the quiz in figure 2.1.

Carefully review the application and résumé prior to the interview. Familiarity with the candidate's application paperwork, so that you do not have to refer to it often during the interview, will allow you to concentrate on asking questions and listening carefully to the candidate's answers.

During the Interview

The climate created in an interview is important. Create a welcoming atmosphere, away from noise and interruptions. Introduce yourself to the candidate. Determine the candidate's preferred name and use it during the interview. Set a tone for a friendly exchange of comments and allow communication to develop freely in order to build mutual confidence.[3]

Describe the position, the work of the unit or department, and the library. Keep in mind that an interview is a two-way process. The candidate needs to know about the position, your department, salary information, training opportunities, and other information that will help him or her make a decision about accepting the position if it is offered. You want to learn as much as possible about the candidate's qualifications for and interest in the position.

Asking applicants for examples from their past work history or educational experiences will reveal areas of knowledge, skills, and abilities required for them to be successful on the job. By the close of the interview, you want to have an accurate and balanced picture of the applicant's qualifications and job motivation. Behavioral, situational, and competency-based interview questions will provide the best information for determining how successful the applicant could be in the position. Your organization may have a set of knowledge, skills, behaviors, and attributes (the components of formal core competencies lists), as well as core values, that is important for the particular position and important to your organization. If you have a defined set of core competencies for your library or unit, it will be important to ask interview questions that will be helpful in determining whether your applicant meets or could meet a level of competency in areas important to your unit. To elicit information about candidates' knowledge, skills, behaviors, and attributes, you should ask questions related to the competencies that are important to the position.

If creativity is a competency, you might ask questions like these:

> Tell me about a way in which you worked with other staff to develop creative ideas to solve problems.
>
> Describe how you've gone about learning a new technical task.
>
> In your current position, what have you done differently from your predecessors?
>
> Tell me about a creative idea you had to improve a library service.
>
> Tell me about a unique approach you took to solve a problem.

If working in groups (teamwork) is important for the position, consider asking these questions:

> Can you give me an example of a group decision you were involved in recently? What did you do to help the group reach that decision?

Describe a time you worked with a group or team to determine project responsibilities. What was your role?

If you value flexibility and adaptability in employees in your unit, you might want to ask questions like these:

Tell me about an important project/task/assignment you were working on in which the specifications changed. What did you do? How did it affect you?

Tell me about a time you had to meet a scheduled deadline while your work was being continually interrupted. What caused you to have the most difficulty and why?

Going from [position] to [position] must have been difficult. Tell me about a challenge that occurred when making that transition. How did you handle it?

Describe a time you had to significantly modify work procedures to align with new strategic directives.

If problem solving is a competency, examples of questions to consider asking include the following:

Walk me through a situation in which you had to get information by asking many questions of several people. How did you know what to ask?

Describe a time you had to ask questions and listen carefully to clarify the exact nature of an internal/external customer's problem.

To determine leadership ability or potential, consider asking these questions:

Tell me about a time you inspired someone to work hard to do a good job.

Describe a face-to-face meeting in which you had to lead or influence a sensitive individual.

Tell me about a time you were able to convince someone from outside [the applicant's department, etc.] to cooperate with you on an important project.

What strategies have you used to communicate a major change to employees? Which strategies have worked and which have not?

Describe a situation in which you had to translate a broad or general plan into specific goals.

For positions where customer service is important, for both internal and external customers, consider asking questions like these:

In your current job, how do you know if customers are satisfied? Give a specific example.

Tell me about a time when you were able to respond to a customer's request in a shorter period of time than expected. Contrast that situation with a time you failed to meet a customer's expectations. What was the difference?

As a [position title], how did you ensure that you were providing good service?

Sometimes it's necessary to work with a customer who has unusual requests. Please describe a time when you had to handle an unusual request that seemed unreasonable. What did you do?

Some days can be very busy with requests from customers and co-workers. Please describe a time recently when you didn't have enough time to completely satisfy a particular customer. How did you handle the situation?

If planning skills are critical to the position, consider asking the following questions:

Walk me through yesterday [or last week] and tell me how you planned the day's [or week's] activities.

What procedure have you used to keep track of items that need attention? Tell me about a time you used that procedure.

What objectives did you set for this year? What steps have you taken to make sure that you're making progress on all of them?

Sometimes deadlines don't allow the luxury of carefully considering all options before making a decision. Please give an example of a time this happened to you. What was the result of your decision?

Tell me about a time you were faced with conflicting priorities. In scheduling your time, how did you determine what was a priority?

To determine the applicant's level of technical knowledge or expertise, consider asking these questions:

> Describe a project, situation, or assignment that challenged your skills as a [position]. What did you do to effectively manage the situation?
>
> Sometimes complex projects require additional expertise. Describe a situation in which you had to request help.
>
> Have you ever had to orient a new employee on a technical task or area? How did you do it?
>
> Describe a time you solved a technical problem.
>
> What equipment have you been trained to operate? How proficient are you?
>
> What software packages can you use? How proficient are you?
>
> Give me an example of a project that demonstrates your technical expertise in [webpage development].
>
> Describe how you've gone about learning a new technical task.
>
> Describe the most challenging work you've done.

To determine the level of a candidate's interpersonal skills, you might want to ask questions like these:

> Working with people from backgrounds or cultures other than your own can present challenges. Can you tell me about a time you faced a challenge adapting to a person from a different background or culture? What happened? What did you do? What was the result?
>
> Our relationships with coworkers are not always perfect. Tell me about the most challenging relationship you had with a coworker. Why was it challenging? What did you do to try to make it work?[4]

In addition to the kinds of questions just outlined, Chris will want to ask specific questions about research data interest and skills. Chris may find that a candidate who is enthusiastic and willing to learn is a better fit for this new venture than someone with a lot of technical skills but poor interpersonal skills. In other words, hire talent and understand that much of the time you can teach skills. Recruiting an enthusiastic learner can be more successful in the long run than hiring someone with experience who does not fit well in the organization, is not a strong collaborator, and is not enthusiastic about the challenge of starting a new project.

During the interview, your job is to listen, ask follow-up questions when necessary, and evaluate the candidate's answers to try to predict future performance. Practice good communication skills, such as active listening, reflecting, and reframing, and you will learn much about the candidate.

If you find the candidate is giving short answers and you are not learning enough about the person, ask follow-up questions. Continue to probe the answers until you feel comfortable that you have learned all you need to from the candidate. Candidates may be nervous, particularly if they are new to the job market. You can help the person relax by asking questions that help him or her explain his or her skills and interests. Do not settle for a "Yes" or "No" answer if you want more information. Ask again if needed. This is your chance to learn about the candidate. Follow-up questions to gain more insight into a candidate's experiences are appropriate. Ask questions and listen carefully.

When you have finished asking your questions, ask the candidate if he or she has any additional information related to the position that he or she would like you to know. This gives the applicant the chance to mention or reiterate any strengths he or she brings to the position. Then ask the candidate if he or she has any questions for you.

If an applicant voluntarily offers information that you would not ask for legal reasons (see the quiz questions in figure 2.1), human resources specialists recommend that you not note the information that the applicant volunteers. Instead, guide the interview back to issues specifically related to the job.

At the end of the interview, thank the applicant for his or her interest in the position, outline the process for what will happen next, and give the applicant a sense of the timeline for the search.

After the Interview

After the interview, note your impressions of the job candidate and his or her answers to the questions you posed. Complete this task as soon as possible after the interview, particularly when you are interviewing multiple applicants.

Once you have completed all the interviews and are assessing the results to decide which candidate best fits the requirements for the position, remember to check applicants' references, if you have not already done so. Many organizations require that supervisors check references prior to making an employment offer. Even if this is not a requirement at your library, never offer a position to a candidate without first checking references.

Reference Checks

Conducting reference checks will give you added insight into an applicant's personal characteristics and past job performance (i.e., experience, reliability, attendance, quality of work) and allow you to verify the information that the candidate provided. Make sure you obtain the applicant's consent before calling a former or current employer. If possible, work with your library's or larger organization's human resources department to revise application forms so as to require applicants to list all previous employers, dates of employment, positions held, names of supervisors, and reasons for departure. It is important to be consistent in conducting all reference checks.

When checking references, keep notes of the people contacted, what questions were asked, and what answers you received. And, as with interview

FIGURE 2.2
Sample Script for a Reference Check

Hello. My name is [your name] and I work at [Such-and-Such Library]. We are interviewing for a [data management librarian position]. [Applicant's name] has given your name as a reference. [Applicant's name] was employed by you from [beginning date] until [ending date].

- What was the nature of his or her job?
- How would you describe the quality of his or her work?
- What are his or her strong points?
- What are his or her weak points?
- How did he or she get along with other people?
- Would you comment on his or her attendance; dependability; ability to take on responsibility; ability to follow instructions; degree of supervision needed; overall attitude; quality of work; quantity of work?
- Why did he or she leave the position?
- Would you reemploy him or her? If no, why not?

Is there anything else you would like to comment on regarding [applicant's name]'s employment or job performance?

questions for applicants, the same questions should be asked of each applicant's references. Developing a standardized form or script can make reference checks systematic and easy to conduct. Use the reference check to verify factual information, such as dates of employment. Figure 2.2 shows a sample script for a reference check.

Background Checks

Increasingly, libraries or the larger organizations to which they report—college or university campuses, city or town governments, and so on—require criminal background checks for all new employees. Some organizations require background checks for certain positions, for example, employees working with children and employees with money-handling responsibilities. Be sure to know the requirements in your organization. Work closely with your human resources office to determine what information is needed for a background check and to ensure that any release forms needed for the information are filled out correctly. Never offer a position until the results of a background check are known. Be sure that any negotiations about the position make it clear that a job offer will be dependent upon the results of the criminal background check.

Negotiating the Offer

When all interviews are finished, comments and input have been collected from all who participated in the interviews, references have been checked, and required background checks have been completed, you are ready for the next step of making the job offer to your top candidate. Prior to contacting the successful candidate, be sure you have all the information you need to make the offer: details on salary, vacation, sick leave, and retirement benefits as well as start date, moving expenses, and whom, besides you, to contact with questions about any of these topics.

For salary, you should know the amount of funding available for the position. In some situations, your organization might have a prescribed salary range for positions at certain levels. Sometimes you may have a specific salary you can offer, with no room for negotiation. If this is a union position, be sure you are aware of union rules for salary levels. If your organization offers some flexibility with salaries, be sure to consider what staff members in the same type of position or at the same level are earning. Look at the candidate's years of experience, additional education, and any other factors that might influence the salary that you can offer to the candidate.

For vacation, holidays, sick leave, retirement, and other benefits, be sure you have all the information you need for your conversation. Your organization will likely have a human resources or personnel office to which you can refer the candidate if he or she has additional questions about these benefits.

Be prepared to suggest a start date, and then be ready to negotiate based on the needs of the candidate. If your search results in a local candidate, someone who lives in the area and will not need to move, you can suggest a start date as soon as you can be ready for the person to start. (See chapter 3 for details on what you will need to be ready on day one.) Depending on the type of position, you may have conducted a national search. In this case, your candidate may be moving from another city across the country and will need more than two weeks to relocate. Know what the ideal start date would be from your unit's perspective, and then be prepared to take into account the needs of your successful candidate. Many libraries offer moving expenses for some library positions, particularly for librarians who are moving from out of town to a new position. Be sure you know the policy of your library before you make a commitment.

Sometimes a search is very successful, giving you more than one acceptable candidate. Rank them in order of preference, with a plan to contact the top choice first. In this fortunate situation, when negotiating an offer with your top candidates, take care to keep the process moving. Give a candidate enough time to make a decision about accepting your offer but not so much time that you lose your next acceptable candidate. Also, keep this part of the search process confidential. If your second-choice candidate ends up joining your organization, you do not want him or her to feel "second best" or for current staff to know that this individual was not your first choice.

Sometimes searches are not successful, leaving you with no viable candidates. When this happens, you may want to review the job advertisement and position description and ask colleagues at other libraries to review it too. Either or both may need a rewrite to bring in different types of candidates. If the ad and job description seem acceptable, you might want to think about reconsidering candidates in the initial pool who were not selected to interview or reopening the search.

Summary

Hiring decisions are some of the most important decisions you will make as a manager or supervisor. You will be most successful when you do the following:

> Carefully think through the requirements of the position and how it contributes to the overall success of the your unit and the library's plans.
>
> Clearly state the job requirements in the position advertisement.
>
> Ask behavioral questions that are job related.
>
> Listen carefully to interviewees.
>
> Hire for talent and train for skills.
>
> Know your own biases and guard against making decisions based on those biases.
>
> Ask legal questions and avoid non-work-related questions.

When you hire the right people for the right jobs, you will have the solid foundation you need for a successful unit or department.

NOTES

1. Scott Page, *The Difference: How the Power of Diversity Creates Better Groups, Firms, Schools, and Societies* (Princeton, NJ: Princeton University Press, 2008).
2. Beth McNeil, "Managing Work Performance and Career Development: Implications for Human Resources in Academic Libraries," in *Human Resource Management in Today's Academic Library: Meeting Challenges and Creating Opportunities*, ed. Janice Simmons-Welburn and Beth McNeil (Westport, CT: Libraries Unlimited, 2004), 57–68.
3. Thyra Russell, "Interviewing," in *Practical Help for New Supervisors*, ed. Joan Giesecke (Chicago: American Library Association, 1997), 6–14.
4. University Libraries, University of Nebraska–Lincoln, internal document on core competency–related interview questions.

3

Orientation and Training

Once the search is over and you have filled the vacancy in your unit, you may believe your work is done. Not quite! Now you must orient the new employee to your library. An effective orientation is critical for employee success and should include introductions to current staff and an introduction to policies and procedures. It also provides an opportunity for the new person to begin to get to know the culture of the organization. The new employee's orientation, in particular the first day on the job, can influence how he or she will feel about the library throughout his or her employment.[1]

The details of an orientation program will vary depending on the type and size of your library as well as the nature of the position. However, many libraries share common goals for new employee orientation, as summarized by H. Scott Davis in his book *New Employee Orientation*, including the following:

> To make all new library employees feel welcome and comfortable as they begin the new job
>
> To provide consistent documentation and interpretation of major library policies and philosophies for all new employees and, in the course of doing so, to strive to avoid "information overload"
>
> To acquaint all new library employees with other library staff and other departments and units within the library system
>
> To provide continuing orientation support to all new employees during the initial months of their employment through mentoring and other activities
>
> To tailor individual orientation activities/information according to the varying information needs for different positions within the library and, in doing so, to be mindful of individual differences among new employees in terms of personal experience and educational background
>
> To emphasize the new employee's role and potential for contributing to the overall mission of the unit/department, division, and library
>
> To call attention to the importance of continuing staff development and the library's commitment to staff training, and to emphasize new employees' share of responsibility in self-initiating/communicating staff development needs to their supervisor[2]

Orientation

Preparation for the orientation of a new employee should start as soon as you have made a hiring decision, if not before. Planning includes both in-house preparation and communication with your new employee. Your library may have a general orientation for all new employees. Check with your supervisor or the library's human resources specialist to find out about the standard orientation procedures in your library.

Before the new employee's first day, you will want to review the position description and the job duties or responsibilities for the position and make any necessary changes. These two documents are crucial to the success of the new employee, so that he or she will know both what is expected and how his or her work fits into the larger organization. Carefully plan how you will explain the position and its duties to the new employee.

Today's organizations may include employees from five different generations, ranging in age from sixteen to seventy and older. You may want to consider generational differences when planning the orientation of a new employee.

Your library may have in place a set list of orientation meetings for new employees. You will want to supplement this with sessions pertinent to the particular position that may include meeting with people outside your library. Depending on the nature of the position, and your library's policies, the orientation period may last anywhere from a few weeks to several months. Some meetings can take place during the first week, and others in subsequent weeks. Some details should be handled on the first day at work. Prior to the new employee's first day on the job, you will want to schedule as many meetings as possible for the new employee to meet with colleagues in the unit and in the library. Figure 3.1 shows a sample first-day schedule for new employees.

FIGURE 3.1
Sample Schedule for an Employee's First Day

Library Assistant, Metadata and Cataloging Unit, College Library

Day 1—Thursday, March 1

8:00 A.M.   Meet Jamie Supervisor at library's entry. Receive introduction to unit: review of orientation schedule; review of personnel policies, department procedures, and other general information.

10:30 A.M.   Take tour of library, led by department colleague.

12:00 P.M.   Have lunch with Supervisor.

1:00 P.M.   Attend unit staff meeting.

2:00 P.M.   Go to library human resources department (for employment paperwork).

2:45 P.M.   Meet library director.

3:00 P.M.   Meet unit manager (related unit).

3:30 P.M.   Meet unit manager (related unit).

4:00 P.M.   Review first day with Supervisor.

5:00 P.M.   End of day one!

FIGURE 3.2

Orientation Checklist for Staff in Technical Services

Technical Services Department Orientation Checklist				
New Employee: **Unit:**		**Position:** **Date:**		
FUNCTION/ACTIVITY	PERSON RESPONSIBLE	1ST DAY	1ST WEEK	SUBSEQUENT WEEKS
Review of orientation schedule				
Review of position description, job duties, and responsibilities				
Review of personnel policies Hours and scheduling Time sheets Breaks Types of leave Staff development programs/training Use of computers and e-mail Other				
Tour of library				
Introduction to e-mail system and log-on				
Individual meetings with unit staff				
Individual meetings with staff in other units Cataloging supervisor Serials manager Binding manager Etc.				
Orientation to computer network				
Employment paperwork				
Keys				
Parking permit				
Online catalog training				

Orientation Checklists

As a supervisor, you may find it helpful to use an orientation checklist for new employees. Your library may have a general checklist you can tailor to your unit's needs. If not, develop one for your unit. The checklist might include people to meet within the unit, the library, and outside the library; meetings to attend; and projects or programs with which to become familiar as soon as possible. The checklist may include the names of those responsible for particular aspects of orientation and whether or not the item or function is required or optional. (See figure 3.2.)

Orientation checklists can be used as a supervisory planning tool prior to the employee's first day of work. They can also serve as the written orientation plan that you give to the new employee during your first meeting with him or her. Some checklists note a time frame for when each meeting or activity should take place. Others are less detailed and serve more as a reminder list of meetings that need to be scheduled, such as the sample list for a new librarian shown in figure 3.3.

FIGURE 3.3
Orientation Checklist for a Research Data Librarian

Schedule meeting with division heads, one each week:

☐ Reference/Instruction   ☐ Information Technology

☐ Collections and Technical Services   ☐ Other: _____

☐ Scholarly Communication

Schedule meeting with one department/unit head each week:

☐ Circulation   ☐ Government Documents

☐ Interlibrary Loan   ☐ Metadata/Cataloging

☐ Media and Microforms   ☐ Other: _____

Regularly scheduled meetings to add to calendar:

☐ Reference department meetings (1st and 3rd Thursdays at 1:00 P.M.)

☐ Scholary Communication team meetings (4th Wednesday at 3:00 P.M.)

☐ Library faculty meetings (1st Tuesday in September, December, February, and May at 9:00 A.M.)

Other meetings to schedule after librarian is on board:

☐ Academic departments

Preparations for Arrival

Prior to the new employee's arrival, prepare his or her work space. Make certain that the basic equipment and office supplies necessary for the position are in place and ready to use. Depending on the position, these might include desk supplies and necessary ergonomic equipment related to extended computer workstation use. Some organizations are moving to a more mobile workforce with traditional supplies available at a convenient centralized location. A checklist of supplies for consideration is included at the end of this chapter.

Last, make arrangements with the new employee regarding what time he or she should report to work on the first day and where you will meet him or her. Share the orientation schedule with the employee prior to his or her first day. If this is not possible, at least provide the new employee with a schedule for his or her first day, with confirmation of where and when he or she should report.

First Day on the Job

Setting the right tone for the new person's first day on the job is crucial. At the end of the first day, the new person should feel welcomed to the unit and library and valued for the skills he or she brings to the job. He or she should know the general plan for orientation and what training to expect in the next few weeks.

A person beginning a new job may be anxious about many things on the first day, including everything from how to remember the names of all the people he or she will meet to the scope of his or her job duties. Your goal is to alleviate that anxiety. When you first meet the new employee, greet the person warmly and welcome him or her to the library. Remind the new employee of your name, and let the person know how to address you:

> Good morning. I'm Jamie Supervisor. It's good to see you again. We're so glad you're joining us here at the library. As I mentioned during your interview, I'm the manager of the metadata/cataloging unit and I will be your supervisor. Please call me Jamie. May I call you [employee's first name]?

If your name is difficult to pronounce, repeat it and, if possible, provide a key to remembering how to pronounce it. For example, on this author's first day

at a new job in a large library several years ago, one of the librarians introduced himself and quickly shared a way to remember how to pronounce his
last name, Mykytiuk. He suggested asking myself, "What did Mickey take?"
and answering, "Mickey took . . ." To this day, I have not forgotten his kind-
ness or how to pronounce his name. Some libraries have policies or practices
regarding staff name tags. If your library culture does not include name tags,
you may want to find a way to help a new employee remember the names of
new colleagues as you make introductions to other staff throughout the day.

Review the orientation and training schedule with the new employee.
Explain with whom he or she will be meeting and the purpose of each
meeting. If possible, include names of meeting attendees on the orientation
and training schedules. Note any regular standing meetings that the new
employee should plan to attend.

Introduce the new person to members of the unit and to other staff with
whom he or she will work frequently. On the first day, these introductions
can be brief. Your orientation schedule will include time for in-depth meetings, and for explaining the staff member's work and his or her role in the
department, later in the orientation period.

The first day on the job should include a tour of the unit or department
and the library. You or another member of the unit can lead the tour. Try to
show the employee as much of the library as possible without overwhelming
him or her. During the tour, you may encounter additional staff members to
introduce to the new employee. Depending on the size of your library, you
may decide to tailor the tour, perhaps saving some parts for future days. In
some large organizations with many new employees, general tours and orientation sessions are scheduled regularly so that new employees can meet other
new people and form a cohort of sorts. Regardless of the size of your library
or unit, at the very minimum, you should make sure your new employee
knows how to find the bathroom and the break room and how to navigate to
the unit from the library's entry and vice versa.

Although you may have shared the position description with the new
employee at the time of the interview, you should review it with him or her
again in detail on the first day. Discuss each job duty, the tasks and routines
associated with it, and how performance on each duty will be evaluated.

At some point during the first day, a new employee will need to work
with your human resources staff to complete appropriate paperwork in order
to ensure timely payment of salary or wages. Some libraries may handle these

details prior to the first day on the job. Check with your human resources specialist to learn the procedures in your library.

Finally, keep in mind that your new employee will need time to become familiar with his or her new work space and to review the documentation that you have shared during the day. This "downtime" will allow the employee an opportunity to reflect on the meetings and activities of his or her first day on the job.

A first day on a new job for any new employee should be informative but not overwhelming. At the end of the day, the new employee should feel welcomed and energized to return the next day to learn more about his or her new position and organization.

Training

Training is an integral part of orientation. During your initial discussions with the new employee, including the review of the orientation schedule and the position documents, the new employee should learn more about the specific training necessary for the position. A focus on training during this initial orientation will signify to the employee that you value his or her ongoing development. Increasingly, the jobs of librarians and library staff members are changing to meet the ever-evolving information needs of library users. Most positions in today's libraries require ongoing training to stay up-to-date with new software versions, Web resources, and other electronic resources. During orientation, it will be important to share with a new staff member your expectations for attendance at staff development and training events.

As a supervisor, you may be responsible for much of the position-specific training for a new employee. As you are considering the content for the training, you may want to think about how to best deliver the training and what to teach the new employee first. Knowing the employee's preferred learning style will help. Questions to consider include these: "Will the content be understood more easily and retained longer if the employee sees a videotape, completes a workbook, or listens to a presentation? In what sequence should new information be presented? What should we teach the new employee first—how to search a book order or how to process a vendor list? Does it matter?"[3]

Many libraries also provide library-wide training for library staff and librarians. Sometimes this training is organized and developed by the library administration or by a staff development committee or team. Training may be on topics such as customer service, facilitation skills, communication skills, basic library skills, leadership development, measurement and assessment, team building, technical skills, or other efforts related to library-wide goals or library administration initiatives. The library administration may encourage, and sometimes require, staff participation at training on issues related to organizational culture. Some libraries have developed training or career development plans tailored to individual staff members. Whether you are developing a single training session to address one topic or a multisession training program for a new employee, effective training programs include the following steps:

1. Analyzing needs
2. Describing the task
3. Analyzing the task
4. Writing objectives
5. Developing tests
6. Formulating instructional strategies
7. Sequencing
8. Developing materials
9. Preparing evaluations[4]

By becoming familiar with the staff development planning and opportunities in your library, you will be able to plan for appropriate orientation and ongoing training for the staff you supervise.

Mentoring

Mentoring is an important aspect of work in libraries that is sometimes overlooked in the planning process for orientation and training. Sometimes libraries or their larger organizations have formal mentoring programs to assist employees throughout their careers. These programs may involve formal pairings of employees, with an experienced employee mentoring a new employee or an employee moving into a new role. Sometimes mentoring relationships develop much less formally, between two people who "click" and agree to be in a mentoring relationship. Sometimes mentoring relationships are short term, with a specific focus or goal to achieve; other times mentoring relationships last for years. As a supervisor, be prepared to serve as mentor to your employees and to help them to develop mentoring relationships with others in your library or in the library field.

Summary

A carefully planned orientation program will help your employees begin their jobs on a positive note and with the information they need to succeed. Remember to include the following in your plans.

BEFORE THE FIRST DAY

Communicate with the employee regarding the logistical issues of the first day on the job: when and where to report, work schedule or hours, where to park, and so on.

Prepare the work area with supplies and arrange for necessary networking and connections.

Pencils, pens
Scissors
Notepads
Wrist rest
Phone books
Staff directory with phone, e-mail,
    and office address information

Stapler
Paper
Mouse pad
Wastebasket
Recycle bin

Assess equipment needs.

Computer workstation
Headphones
Network/intranet permissions

Printer
Flash drive or thumb drive

FIRST DAY

Meet and welcome new employee.

Introduce employee to coworkers.

Provide tour of library.

Review job duties and responsibilities.

Explain e-mail, phone access, staff intranet, and other shared drives.

Complete employment paperwork.

FIRST WEEK

Discuss and review unit or department policies.

Provide follow-up tours, depending on size of library.

Discuss library goals and objectives and library-wide policies.

Provide training in core job areas.

SUBSEQUENT WEEKS

Meet with pertinent staff members and departments.

Provide ongoing training.

NOTES

1. Katherine Branch, "Orienting the New Library Employee," in *Practical Help for New Supervisors*, ed. Joan Giesecke (Chicago: American Library Association, 1997), 15–23.
2. H. Scott Davis, *New Employee Orientation: A How-To-Do-It Manual for Librarians* (New York: Neal-Schuman, 1994), x.
3. Pat L. Weaver-Meyers, "Creating Effective Training Programs," in *Staff Development: A Practical Guide*, 3rd ed., ed. Elizabeth Fuseler Avery, Terry Dahlin, and Deborah Carver (Chicago: American Library Association, 2001), 125.
4. Ibid., 125–28.

4

Managing Performance

Do you enjoy your own performance evaluation conference? Have you received an evaluation that made you feel inspired to continue to do a good job? Or do you approach the annual evaluation session with the same reluctance many of us approach a visit to the dentist? Why do evaluations seem so painful for supervisors and employees? How can you as a supervisor create a process so that an annual performance appraisal is viewed as a positive event in your unit?

A good performance appraisal system begins with a clear understanding between the employee and the supervisor about the parameters of the job, the performance expectations, the rewards for successful performance, and an understanding of what will happen if performance standards are not met.[1] A clear position description that includes standards and expectations for each task is crucial. Clear expectations will help new employees understand what they need to do to succeed. Clear expectations also lay the foundation for any actions you may take to reward employees or to address performance concerns. From a legal perspective, demonstrating consistency in defining, monitoring, and evaluating performance is important. Clear job descriptions and standards provide you with the road map you need to demonstrate consistency. Standards also protect both new supervisors and experienced managers from applying expectations in an arbitrary and subjective manner. Rewarding one employee and not another when both meet a given standard will lead to problems for a supervisor. At a minimum, you will be seen as inconsistent and can lose the respect of your unit. At the extreme, you may be guilty of discrimination and could face legal action.

Performance appraisal does not need to be a legal quagmire. Instead of approaching the issue of performance appraisal as an awful annual burden, try to see this aspect of management as an opportunity to work with the staff in your unit to make the unit excel. How can you do this?

Standards and Expectations

One of the first steps in the process of establishing a positive performance appraisal system and experience is to enlist the participation of your staff in setting standards and expectations. First, learn about your organization's standards and processes. Share these standards with the staff in your unit. Then work with each employee to determine how the standards will apply to his or her work. Depending on the nature of the position, there may be quantifiable goals to be met, or some aspects of the position may need more qualitative measures to determine success. For example, if your organization has a customer service standard that no more than three legitimate customer complaints per year will be considered satisfactory, then discuss how you will assess a complaint. If a patron yells at a staff member at the desk because the staff member is following a policy the person does not like, as a supervisor, you may establish that this type of incident does not constitute a legitimate complaint. However, if the staff member yells back or uses inappropriate language, that would be a legitimate complaint against the staff member. Outlining these types of expectations before an incident occurs will give you a foundation for rewarding positive behavior (staff member did not yell) or addressing negative behavior (staff member did yell). If your organization does not have standards in place for a particular task or position, then you have the opportunity to develop or revise the standards with your staff. Including staff in the discussion will help them both understand and accept the standards you develop. The input from staff must be taken seriously. If you are asking for input only because you think you should and have no intention of using the staff input, staff will quickly become disillusioned and will see you as arbitrary rather than supportive.

Staff and managers may declare that quantitative expectations do not apply to their positions, that too much of what they do is subjective and cannot be measured. This argument often comes from the more public-facing areas, such as reference work, or in describing supervisory roles. In these cases, more qualitative standards or outcomes may be needed. For example, for a fund-raising or public relations position, the outcome of an encounter with a donor or with the media may be beyond a person's control. Nevertheless, setting expectations, such as writing thank-you notes within two days of a visit or interview, will allow you, as a supervisor, to describe the behaviors the person does control and to evaluate those actions.

In larger organizations where a number of people perform similar tasks, developing standards and expectations helps to create organization-wide expectations. With generic standards in place, the organization is more likely to treat staff consistently across units. The more an organization can show that staff are treated consistently for similar work, the better. Staff morale will improve, and there will be less opportunity for the organization to be found guilty of discrimination.

Generic standards should describe duties and tasks, expectations, and the impact of these standards. The standards should be understandable, clear, and meaningful. For example, a generic statement of responsibility for supervisors might look like the one presented in figure 4.1. The responsibilities listed there are required for a well-functioning and productive unit. A generic statement of duties with expectations for a time and attendance clerk could resemble the one shown in figure 4.2. The challenge for you as a new supervisor is to be as specific as possible in writing standards while not becoming so detailed that the person feels like a cog in a wheel. Staff need direction that contributes to the process of planning their workflow, rather than step-by-step instructions that take away all need for a person to think.

FIGURE 4.1

Supervise the [Such-and-Such] Unit, consisting of [number] FTE (full-time equivalent) staff

Work with the human resources department to develop replacement ads for open positions.

Conduct job searches for vacant positions, including interviewing.

Make recommendations for hiring staff.

Establish performance expectations and develop position descriptions, reviewing and updating them annually or as needed.

Train staff or ensure that training occurs.

Evaluate progress and performance, offer support, and coach or mentor staff to meet library core competencies.

Meet regularly, both formally and informally, with staff.

Document performance issues.

Prepare written and oral evaluations of staff in the unit and conduct annual and probationary evaluations.

Recommend salary adjustments.

In consultation with supervisor and library administration, conduct disciplinary action or recommend termination for staff when necessary.

Follow all library personnel policies. Attend training programs offered by the human resources department and the library to acquire an essential knowledge of personnel policies.

Impact statement

Strong supervisory and management skills are vital for the smooth operation of the unit, for maintaining a welcoming environment for all staff, and for maintaining a positive library image to the public.

Plan and manage workflow of the Unit, consisting of [number] FTE staff and [number] FTE student assistants.

Develop unit goals and expectations in consultation with others as appropriate.

Develop and review policies and procedures. Recommend and execute changes as needed.

Create written documentation of routines and procedures.

Conduct unit meetings.

Schedule specific job duties, vacations, and so on for the unit.

FIGURE 4.2

Sample Statement of Responsibility for a Time and Attendance Clerk

Time cards

Serve as time and attendance clerk for staff. Review time cards on a biweekly basis, checking for accuracy and completeness. Check for staff signature, total the regular work hours and leave hours, enter correct payroll earnings codes, and sign off on time cards. Send all time cards to the library administration before the appropriate deadline.

Serve as time and attendance clerk for student assistants. Compare time cards against work schedule and bring any discrepancy to the attention of the supervisor. Check time cards for accuracy and completeness. Check for student signature, total the work hours, and sign student time cards. Enter student totals on student payroll sheet. Send all time cards and payroll sheets to the library administration before the appropriate deadline.

Maintain current knowledge of payroll and timekeeping procedures.

Impact statement

Accuracy ensures correct salary payments for hours worked and that time and attendance reporting is correct. Inaccurate reporting will violate library policies. Meeting deadlines allows the library administration to record payments and in turn allows the Payroll Office to process salary payments on time.

SOURCE: Adapted from the University of Nebraska–Lincoln Libraries' NU Values generic statements, 2003.

Standards and expectations should be reviewed regularly, at least annually, to be sure they are still relevant to the work and the unit. For example, a change in systems or software programs can result in a change in workflow that then impacts expectations. Unless the expectations are reviewed regularly, they can become less applicable as the environment changes.

Performance Evaluation Systems

Once job descriptions and standards and expectations are in place, you have the beginning of a performance evaluation system. Now is not the time to put these documents away, only to drag them out in a year to see how staff are doing. Instead, these need to be documents you work with and refer to throughout the year. First, verify that the staff are clear about job duties and expectations. For new employees, you need to review this information during the orientation process. Then follow up with employees every few months to be sure they understand how the expectations apply to their positions. In some organizations, the human resources manager will schedule a ninety-day review with each new employee to discuss the expectations and be sure the employee understands the job. Having someone outside the unit do this review can help unearth misunderstandings the supervisor could miss. For all employees, standards and expectations should be reviewed semiannually to ensure that changes in performance are addressed early and that any needed changes in expectations are handled quickly.

It is very important that the supervisor clearly communicate changes in policies and procedures as these changes occur. There should be no surprises during annual performance reviews. Do not wait for a formal performance review to tell a staff member that the organization's policy has changed.

It is not fair to hold an employee accountable for following a change in policy or procedure if that change has not been clearly communicated to the staff. Sending out a written notice of the change may not be sufficient to guarantee that all employees are fully aware of it. Reviewing changes at a department or unit meeting may be more effective because it will allow employees to ask questions about the changes. This way, both the supervisor and the employees can be sure they understand the changes, know why the changes have occurred, and have reviewed how the changes impact the unit.[2]

Ongoing Discussion

Discussing job performance can be built into a regular routine with each staff member so that you are keeping communication lines open in your unit. A supervisor should have a fairly formal meeting every two to four weeks with each staff member to review how the job is going, to answer any questions that have arisen, and to ensure that, as a supervisor, you know how your staff are doing. These meetings can be informal in tone but should always give the staff member a chance to report progress and discuss issues. It is also a time when, as a supervisor, you can address any questions or concerns you have. With regular meetings, you can avoid unpleasant surprises and can help staff stay on course. This is a time to recognize good work, praise staff for successes, and agree to new projects or objectives.

Annual Performance Appraisal

Jamie sits down to write his first evaluations for his new staff, most of whom were previously his colleagues. Most of the staff are performing well. Jamie knows, however, that Tom has never been a stellar performer, and Jamie is surprised to discover there is no documentation to show that Tom is chronically late for work and has not met performance standards. Jamie realizes he must begin a process to alert Tom to these issues and develop a plan for Tom to improve his performance.

Jamie is frustrated because he knows this has been going on for years and yet no supervisor before him has been willing to document the issues. Jamie can find no written record that Tom has been notified that there is a problem with his performance. Jamie must begin from scratch.

He notes that the metadata/cataloging unit has performance standards and that he has compared the performance standards to Tom's annual report. Jamie notes that there is a gap between the standards and what Tom has reported. Jamie writes that he will work with Tom this year to develop a plan to improve his performance.

Jamie does not note the chronic lateness problem because there is no written standard that he can apply in this evaluation. Jamie assigns Tom an evaluation rating of "needs improvement." Jamie knows that Tom will be upset, and so he carefully prepares for the oral conference. He plans to provide a copy of the department's performance standards and acknowledge that Tom has not been given the standards before. He anticipates the questions that Tom might ask. Jamie plans to ask Tom if he feels he is meeting the performance expectations and then how he thinks he can improve his performance to meet expectations. If Tom does not have ideas, Jamie is prepared to begin a discussion of planning for change. While Jamie knows this will not be an easy evaluation, he is confident he is beginning a process in sync with his institution's human resources procedures: giving Tom notice he needs to improve, developing with Tom a plan for improving, giving Tom time to improve, and establishing a paper trail in case Tom's performance does not improve.

Most organizations will have a system for annual performance evaluations. The process may include a standardized form and a rating system, or the system may use open-ended letters, leaving the process up to the supervisor. No matter what system you use, a good supervisor will write a clear analysis of the staff member's performance. Vague statements will not be helpful to the staff member, nor will it provide the employee with any advice on what is working well. Present a balanced view of the staff member's performance, noting strengths and accomplishments. Emphasizing strengths will help a staff member focus on successes and will help provide a more motivating environment. A performance evaluation is also a means to document any concerns about a person's performance. Again, balance is a key. Do not overemphasize recent experiences or ignore past events. The evaluation should reflect the entire year.

To complete a successful performance evaluation, follow these steps:

1. Review the staff member's position description, standards, and expectations. Be sure you know what the employee is supposed to be doing.

2. Review your notes on the person's performance for the year. Identify major successes and areas of outstanding performance. Note, too, any areas that need improvement.

3. Complete the evaluation form or write the evaluation letter. Be sure to focus on the current year's performance. Note improvements from the last evaluation. Do not raise past issues that have been resolved more than a year ago. Tie performance to expectations so that the staff member knows how the work he or she has done is reflected in the evaluation.

4. Be consistent. The evaluation should contain no surprises. If you have not addressed a problem this year, you should not blame the staff member for not improving. You may list this as an area for growth, but it should not adversely affect a staff member's overall rating.

5. Once the form is complete, give it to the staff member to review prior to any discussion about performance. Some organizations will specify how many workdays the staff member has to review a written evaluation prior to an oral conference. Carefully follow your organization's procedures.

6. Plan the oral conference. Do not read the written form to the employee. Rather, decide on strengths to highlight, accomplishments to review, and concerns to discuss.

7. At the oral conference, outline strengths. Note areas of improvement. Answer any questions the staff member may have. Listen carefully to his or her concerns. Be sure to address any uncertainty, disagreements, or confusion.

8. Review any concerns you have about the person's performance. Discuss plans to address these concerns.

9. Discuss goals and objectives for the coming year. Include plans to address concerns but also ways to build on the staff member's strengths to improve performance and reach excellence. Some organizations tackle this step of goal setting outside the performance discussion, either before or after the conclusion of the annual performance evaluation.

10. Close the conference by signing forms as needed. Articulate any follow-up that is planned.

11. Because performance evaluations are confidential personnel papers, be sure to file the forms as outlined in your organization's procedures immediately after the oral conference. Do not carelessly leave evaluation forms lying around your office. You must keep them safe.[3]

Once the conference is completed and the forms are safely processed, do not ignore performance issues for a year. Do follow-up as needed. Meet regularly with your staff, discuss their accomplishments, and review areas for growth.

Academic Environment and Tenure Systems

Some academic libraries have the added layer of an academic rank-and-tenure framework for their librarians, in addition to an annual evaluation process. When these two systems are well integrated, librarians and library faculty members have a sound understanding of all the components of their positions, including librarianship/teaching, research/scholarship, and service/outreach/extension, and they know how they will be evaluated on their progress. When the promotion and tenure process is separate from the annual evaluation process, it can result in confusion and difficulty for supervisors when they address performance issues. If you are supervising tenure-track librarians, be sure to understand both campus and library policies relating to tenure and promotion.

Unions

Libraries in union environments may have specific processes and policies relating to performance evaluation and merit salary increases. In some libraries all staff are unionized, while in other situations only certain groups of staff belong to unions. Unions can be in public, academic, and other types of libraries. As a supervisor, be sure you know the union situation in your library and become familiar with union policies relating to position classification, compensation, and so on. Communicate regularly with your library administration and union representatives about issues of concern.

Performance Problems

When issues of performance do arise, you need to address them quickly. For example, explaining to a staff member that he or she missed a field on a metadata or cataloging record or was late to log on to a chat reference shift is most meaningful close to the event, so you are both clear about the actions that were taken. Waiting too long to discuss concerns about behavior will mean the staff member and you will be less clear about the details of the issue in question.

Although you should address issues as they arise, you also need to take a moment to plan your conversation with the staff member. It is never appropriate to yell at a staff member, whether in the presence of others or not, unless the person is doing something that is potentially self-injurious or hazardous or dangerous to others.

To address a performance issue, follow these steps:

1. First, clarify in your own mind the behavior you want to see from the staff member. Review the standards and expectations for the task in question so you can assess the situation as objectively as possible.

2. Gather facts about the staff member's performance. For example, if attendance is an issue, know how many times the person was late and how that number compares to the standards and expectations.

3. Analyze the facts to determine if the problem can be prevented, if the employee has enough information to do the task, or if the task is too large for one person to do. For example, if you have not trained a staff member to select vendors for ordering books, you cannot fault the person if he or she does not make choices that are appropriate.

4. Set up a meeting with the employee and develop an outline of what you want to accomplish. Be sure you are clear about the behavioral issues you want to address. Have examples and documentation handy so you can be as objective and clear as possible.

5. Hold the meeting with the staff member. Outline your concern using the facts you have gathered. Be direct and clear. You can tell someone he or she was late three days out of five without being insulting.

6. Ask the employee for his or her perspective. How does the staff member think he or she is doing? Does the person acknowledge the problem? Does the person understand the task and how to accomplish the work?

7. With the staff member, develop a plan for improvement. Agree to what changes will be needed to resolve the problem. Set a time to follow up on the issue and review progress.

8. Hold a follow-up session. Has the behavior improved? Are expectations being met? If performance has improved, you and the staff member have been successful in addressing performance. Monitor his or her work as you would for any other staff member to be sure performance remains satisfactory.[4]

What do you do if performance has not improved? How can you address continued performance issues without getting discouraged? First, find out about your organization's procedure for progressive discipline. Most organizations will have a step-by-step process for you to follow. Often, the process begins with an oral warning about the problem. Document when you have this conversation, and be sure the employee knows the conversation is an oral warning. If a person is coming in to work late, telling the person that he or she needs to watch his or her attendance without giving specifics will not be sufficient to serve as the beginning of a disciplinary process. You need to be clear about what is expected and what will happen if the performance does not improve. Be sure to inform your human resources office and provide updates throughout the process.

The next step is a written warning. Here you document the problem and provide a written copy to the staff member. In writing, outline the time frame for addressing the problem and the next steps if the performance does not improve.

Meet regularly to review progress. Employees having problems will need guidance and attention from you to be sure they know when they are making progress. If behavior does not change or the problem is not fixed, document this so you have enough information to move to the next steps in the process.

If performance does not improve, you may have to recommend that a person be terminated. If you reach this point of the process, be sure you work with your organization's human resources office, your supervisor, and any union representatives that are part of the process.

Termination

When a staff member does not meet expectations, is not doing the job that needs to be done, and you have documented your efforts to correct the problem, you need to recommend that the person be terminated. It will not be healthy for the unit or your library organization if you tolerate poor performance. When supervisors do so, others in the unit are forced to do the work of the inadequate staff member. This will build resentment toward you as supervisor, and you can lose the respect of your entire unit.

Termination, though, takes careful planning.[5] Be sure you have followed all of your organization's policies and procedures, reviewed any pertinent labor agreements, and alerted appropriate officials to the situation. Pick a time to meet with the employee. Many superiors will plan the meeting for the end of the day so the employee can leave the workplace at the end of the meeting.

Because terminating a staff member can be an emotional time, you will want to be sure you have arranged a secure, safe location for the meeting.

Determine whether security is needed and, if so, have someone available during the meeting. The night before, be sure all computer work the person has been doing is backed up. Arrange to have passwords and access codes changed as the meeting concludes. You need to protect the unit and the organization should the employee try to harm the organization.

The meeting with the employee can include your supervisor or a representative from your organization's human resources department. Be sure to have at least one person with you to help document the meeting and to help keep the meeting under control.

During the meeting, follow these steps:

1. Briefly review the problems. Do not go into great detail because you do not want to prolong the meeting, nor do you want to make the employee feel worse than needed.

2. Briefly review the steps taken to address the problems.

3. Tell the person that he or she is being terminated, what if any pay he or she will receive, and how to get his or her personal items out of the office. Be as specific as you can be about the arrangements and still be brief.

For example, if a staff member has failed to maintain a schedule, you might say the following:

> [Employee's name], you and I have met eight times over the past two months to discuss your schedule. You are expected to be at work by 8:30 A.M. You have been arriving fifteen to thirty minutes late over 75 percent of the time. Because you have failed to meet expectations and have been unable to correct the problem, we are notifying you that today is your last day of work. You will receive two weeks' severance pay. Our human resources head will accompany you to your desk so you can pack up your things and leave.

The employee may become emotional, may declare the process is unfair, or may do very little. You should be careful not to debate the process with the employee and to stay as calm as possible. Once the employee has regained his or her composure, have someone escort the employee to his or her desk to help him or her pack. Alternately, you may make arrangements for the employee to pack his or her belongings after work hours. In any case, follow your organization's routine and procedures for these situations.

Remember, this meeting is not about you. Avoid telling the staff member how bad you feel or how hard it is for you to fire someone. The staff member is unlikely to care how you feel and could resent you for focusing on your feelings instead of the staff member's situation. Be empathetic and professional as you conduct the meeting.

While terminating an employee is an unpleasant task for a supervisor, if you have followed the organization's procedures, tried to work with the staff member, and been clear about the consequences of not meeting expectations, termination is the expected outcome. Remember that you tried your best to resolve the issue.

When performance is a regular topic of discussion, it becomes less burdensome to you and to the staff member. The discussion becomes a way to improve on performance and to encourage staff growth. The annual evaluation becomes a time to reflect on past accomplishments and plan future directions. When an evaluation is part of an ongoing performance management process, there will be no surprises and your and your employees' attitudes about the annual evaluation process will be more positive and focused on looking forward.

Summary

Performance appraisal begins with a clear job description and understandable standards and expectations. Performance discussions should be an ongoing part of your regular communication with your staff. Address issues quickly. Give praise and recognition regularly. Annual performance appraisals can be a productive time to discuss goals and objectives. They do not need to be a painful, burdensome process. While terminating an employee can be painful, if you carefully follow your organization's rules and procedures, you can make the process less difficult for everyone involved.

NOTES

1. Gary McClain and Deborah S. Romaine, *The Everything Managing People Book* (Avon, MA: Adams Media, 2002), 177.
2. Joan Giesecke, "Appraising Performance," in *Practical Help for New Supervisors*, ed. Joan Giesecke (Chicago: American Library Association, 1997), 26–27.
3. Ibid., 30–31.
4. Ibid., 27–29.
5. McClain and Romaine, *The Everything Managing People Book*, 177.

Managing Rewards

Finding ways to reward employees, beyond the traditional reward structure of salaries and wages, has never been easy. Sometimes library budgets are determined by the larger organization (college or university, school board, library board, etc.), and supervisors may have little control over how extra funds are determined and distributed. Organizations may have policies that limit a supervisor's ability to creatively provide nonmonetary incentives.

Salaries and Monetary Incentives

Policies for how salaries are distributed may be determined outside of the library,

FIGURE 5.1

Incentive Award Policy

The Guiding Principles of Incentive Awards
for the University Libraries

UNIVERSITY OF NEBRASKA–LINCOLN

Link Incentive Awards to the Libraries' mission and goals. Incentive Award decisions must support the University Libraries' goals and values.

Base on prospective or future performance. Incentive Awards are given for prospective work and reward objective, measurable outcomes.

Provide equity in the distribution of Incentive Awards. All regular employees in the Office/Service and Managerial/Professional classifications should be given equal opportunity to be rewarded for the results of their work. Faculty members are not eligible to receive Incentive Awards.

Give Incentive Awards for specific achievements. Actions that produce positive results, rather than subjective feelings and visibility, should be rewarded.

Hold supervisors accountable for using Incentive Awards to achieve or recognize results. Employees feel strongly that supervisors should be responsible for ensuring recognition is linked to positive actions and contributions.

Give Incentive Awards in a timely manner. Employees feel that recognition given in a timely manner is most effective.

Encourage both individual and group Incentive Awards. Group awards encourage teamwork and foster the cooperation needed to address the many complex issues faced by the Libraries.

Give employees a choice in the type of Incentive Award. Whenever possible, recipients should be allowed a choice in the type of award they receive.

Publicize Incentive Awards. The Libraries must be open in publicizing who receives Incentive Awards.

Provide flexibility for Incentive Award programs at the department level.

Provide training for supervisors and staff in effective use of Incentive Awards. A discussion of the recognition process should be included with training for new supervisors.

Periodically monitor and evaluate the Incentive Award program. Report and keep statistics on an annual basis.

Incentive Award programs are subject to change or discontinuation at the option of the University Libraries and/or the University of Nebraska–Lincoln.

Remember that for any reward to be successful, you want to be sure it is tied to performance. You will find that you see the behaviors you reward. Be sure you reward the behaviors that you want to see in your unit.

they may be part of a union contract, or they may be part of an overall organizational system. As a supervisor, you will want to know if people are rewarded for performance in the form of merit increases or if raises are automatic, as in cost-of-living increases or increases based on seniority, or if your organization uses a combination of these depending on staff rank, classification, and unionization. If performance is the basis for merit increases, then be sure you are conducting appropriate performance appraisals, documenting good performance as well as performance problems. Be fair to your staff by making sure that you follow organizational rules in performance procedures, so that your staff will qualify for and be recognized with merit salary increases.

Salary increases alone are not sufficient to serve as monetary rewards and incentives for encouraging and celebrating good performance. As a supervisor, you will want to explore what other options you have for recognizing outstanding performance, celebrating success, and encouraging each employee to do the best he or she can.

Some libraries will have reward structures, incentives, or bonus plans and awards already in place. Check to see if your library has policies on rewarding employees. See figure 5.1 for an example of an incentive award policy.

Review staff award options that exist and remember to nominate your staff for awards when appropriate. Even if staff are not selected, many staff will be pleased that you took the initiative to submit a nomination and feel honored by the recognition.

Nonmonetary Rewards

In times of tight budgets or budget cuts, rewarding employees with monetary awards may not be possible. When funding is an issue, consider nonmonetary rewards.

There are many examples of nonmonetary rewards that you can use to recognize your employees (see figure 5.2). Not all rewards will fit with your organization. Look for rewards that blend well with library policies and unit culture. Nonmonetary rewards can include such efforts as flexible scheduling, job design, celebrations, and awards.[1]

Flexible scheduling. Flexible scheduling allows employees to plan work schedules around other factors in their lives. With many libraries open more than forty hours per week, staff may have a variety of options available to

FIGURE 5.2
Noncash Incentive Rewards

- Time off with pay (one to forty hours)
- Tickets to a local performance (may include movie, theater, sports event, etc.)
- Gift certificates
- Computer accessories, software, or equipment
- Office equipment
- Professional development funds
- Parking permit for one year
- Campus recreation membership
- Other choices to be determined by the employee, supervisor, and library director
- Flexible scheduling (flextime, flexitour, variable day, variable week, etc.)
- Job design (job rotation and job enrichment or enlargement)
- Celebrations of milestones on the job
- Providing desirable committee appointments or related assignments
- Asking the employee to represent the library at professional functions
- Asking the employee to accompany you to appropriate business meetings
- Extending an invitation to coauthor a publication or to work jointly on a special initiative

them to schedule their workweek. When this option is available, work with staff to find schedules that match both staff needs and unit needs. Finding a schedule that works for you, your staff member, and your unit can help a staff member feel valued and be more productive, leading to an overall increase in staff morale.

Job design. Job enrichment, job sharing, and job rotation are all options you can use to give a person new challenges and help him or her learn new skills. In job enrichment, a staff member may take on new responsibilities or special projects. These challenges may be assigned as recognition of outstanding performance on the basic job tasks. In job rotation, staff may exchange positions for a limited time to have the opportunity to try new tasks. In job sharing, two staff may share a position or set up tasks so that they have time to handle other duties or work part-time. In reviewing job design options, be sure you offer opportunities fairly to your staff and do not show favoritism. Ideally, everyone who is performing well should have an opportunity to try

FIGURE 5.3

Sample Staff Award: Iowa State University Library Card

Give Someone an ISU Library Card!

The program was introduced to staff in December 2014 and the first drawing took place in January 2015. The awards committee draws one card randomly from those written for the month. Committee members make their way to the office of the recipient, who gets to choose a gift from the prize vault (an ISU Cyclones bag). The other people who had cards written about them receive a small gift to acknowledge their efforts too.

Impressive. **S**tupendous. **U**ncommon.

Laudable. **i**nvaluable. **b**rilliant. **r**emarkable. **a**wesome. **r**efreshing. **y**ou!

Give someone an ISU Library Card! In a few seconds, you can have a positive effect on the course of someone's day. Spend a little time thinking about what a simple compliment does for your own outlook, then spend a little time thinking about what a little acclaim would do for someone else. In the interest of keeping it informal, take a moment to notice when you see a colleague or coworker doing a little something . . . Impressive. Stupendous. Uncommon. Laudable. invaluable. brilliant. remarkable. awesome. refreshing. you! . . . Then it's as easy as 1 . . . 2 . . . 3 . . . :

1. Identify the person and write your thought/observation on the Impressive. Stupendous. Uncommon. Laudable. invaluable. brilliant. remarkable. awesome. refreshing. you! (ISU Library) card.

2. You DON'T have to identify yourself, but you may if you choose.

3. Pin it to the bulletin board in the Staff Lounge kitchen.

That's it. We hope you will see that a simple gesture can be very influential. At the end of the month, we will gather the cards and draw one. The person mentioned on the drawn ISU Library card will receive a prize. Those who have a card written about them will receive a memento of the occasion.

those different task options. If you are supervising in a union environment, take care to ensure that union rules allow flexibility with job design.

Celebrations. One way to recognize outstanding performance is to celebrate successes. Celebrations can range from elaborate recognition ceremonies to a quick unit coffee break to saying thank-you to a staff member or team. While formal events provide a more structured approach that recognizes unusual efforts, quick celebrations can be a timely way to help staff understand that outstanding effort will be recognized.

Awards. Many libraries have annual recognition awards to acknowledge staff excellence. These awards highlight the accomplishments of staff throughout the year and over time. Learn the criteria for these awards and share them with your staff so they can see how they can qualify for these awards.

Within the unit, you and your staff can create ways to recognize one another's work. Giving awards for new ideas, for suggestions that improve workflow, or for ideas that save money are just a few ways you can show staff that you value their efforts. Figures 5.3 and 5.4 show two examples of ways staff can acknowledge the work of others in the unit or library.

FIGURE 5.4
Sample Staff Award: SMILE

Libraries SMILE Program

Mission Statement
The SMILE (Staff Morale In the Libraries Environment) Program is intended to acknowledge and demonstrate immediate and spontaneous appreciation for the contributions of individuals.

Form of Awards
The SMILE will take two concurrent forms:

1. A thank-you note from a colleague
2. A chance to win an award each month

Submission Process
All submissions are electronic. Submissions are processed by using the Submit button on the SMILE SUBMISSIONS FORM on the staff intranet. The staff member who wrote the note will receive a confirmation receipt. The Libraries Human Resources Coordinator will then copy and paste the information into a personalized e-mail to the recipient and assign the SMILE submission a sequential number that will be used in the random drawing for the monthly award. Anonymous SMILE forms and forms with no information about why the SMILE is being sent will not be accepted.

Award Schedule

The SMILE program took effect on October 1, 2012. There is no set schedule for the distribution of a SMILE, in the form of the personalized thank-you note, as they are intended to be spontaneous. Staff is encouraged to complete a thank-you note in a timely manner to recognize the efforts of others. Thank-you notes received by Human Resources by the last working day of the month will be entered into that month's drawing, to take place on the first working day of the following month (e.g., nominations received by October 31st will be entered into the October pool, the drawing for which will take place on the first business day of November).

Award Amounts

Awards, in the form of gift certificates from the Dean of Libraries, will total $25.00 per award. One award will be given per month.

Award Opportunities

All Libraries' full-time and part-time staff and faculty will have access to the SMILE, both in terms of demonstrating appreciation of others and receiving appreciation from others. (The program does not include undergraduate students and graduate assistants.) An individual receiving multiple thank-you notes per month will have multiple entries in the monthly pool. An individual may receive only one award per fiscal year. The Dean, Associate Deans, and Human Resources Coordinator may receive a SMILE but will not be entered in the drawing.

Selection Process

SMILE thank-you notes for each month will be numbered sequentially, according to the order in which they are received by Human Resources. The monthly drawing for gift certificates will take place on the first business day of each month for the previous month's awards. The Human Resources Coordinator will hold a random drawing from a bag of numbered slips of paper, with each number representing a SMILE submitted in the past month.

Program Facilitation

The Human Resources Coordinator will be responsible for the facilitation of the program, including communication efforts, maintaining supplies of award notes and gift certificates, thank-you note distributions, maintenance of program website, and communication about the program.

Program Communication

The Human Resources Coordinator will submit a monthly message to INSIDe announcing the SMILE recipient for that month. Each issue of INSIDe will also feature a link to the submission form. At the beginning of each semester, a reminder will be submitted to INSIDe as well. Information about SMILE is accessible via the intranet.

Submit a SMILE!

Used with permission from the Purdue University Libraries.

Be sure that you do not overuse awards. You want to promote and recognize desired behaviors, be sure that the performance warrants a reward, and try not to give everyone an award every month.

Generational Issues and Rewards

Changes in the demographics of the workforce complicate the reward structure. Traditional rewards may no longer motivate all employees. Recognizing and understanding generational differences may help you, in your supervisory role, to provide meaningful monetary and nonmonetary rewards for employees.

Writers and researchers on multigenerational differences have varying opinions on the number of generations currently living and the characteristics that distinguish them. The generation of people born before 1924, largely no longer members of the workforce, are often called Matures. The Veteran Generation, born between 1925 and 1945, is also known as the World War II Generation and Traditionalists; many Veterans have retired, but others are still working. Baby Boomers, or Boomers, were born between 1946 and 1963. Sometimes people born between 1962 and 1965 are called Cuspers because they were born in the years overlapping Baby Boomers and Generation X. Generation X, referring to those born between 1964 and 1979, is sometimes called the 13th Generation. Generation Y members were born between 1980 and 1994 and have many names: Millennials, Generation Why?, Echo Boomers, 14th Generation, Y2Kids, Internet Generation, NetGeners or N-Gen, and Netizens. Members of Generation Z, born after 1994, are now working in libraries.[2]

Although the year ranges may shift slightly, and names and titles vary, library employees currently belong to one of the five main generational groups: Veterans, Baby Boomers, Generation X, Generation Y, and Generation Z.

Libraries, like other organizations and businesses, employ staff in all five generations. Employers need to reconsider the traditional reward structure, adjusting to the increasingly Gen X and Gen Y workforce. While generational differences may influence the rewards desired by your employees, be careful not to let the stereotypes of each group determine reward options. Balancing the reward needs of five generations sounds impossible, but it does not have to be. Ask your staff what motivates them. You may be surprised by their answers.

Some workers—for example, those born after 1963—might appreciate nonmonetary incentives or rewards such as increased responsibility, exposure to decision makers, or more control over their own schedules.[3] Adding supervision of student workers to a staff person's job description may be a reward to an employee wanting to build his or her skill set. An informal meeting with the library director and the chance to tell the director about his or her new idea for streamlining the e-journal cataloging process might be greatly appreciated by an employee in a large library. The opportunity to work from home one day a week or to work a nontraditional schedule (10:00 A.M. to 7:00 P.M. instead of 8:00 A.M. to 5:00 P.M.) may help retain a high performer during years of lean raises.

If funding is available, consider purchasing rewards for these employees rather than distributing a cash bonus. Gen X and Gen Y employees may view additional training opportunities as a very worthwhile reward. If the training is job related, the library will benefit as well. Advanced software or the latest computing equipment, which is job related and which the employee would enjoy learning about and using, could also benefit the library. For example, providing the latest mobile or wearable device for a library staff member working in your media lab so that he or she can use the latest Web technologies would be a great reward. The employee gains a new device for personal and work use, and you gain a happy employee with experience using the tools that your library patrons are also using.

Research suggests that Gen Y employees want to feel that their work has meaning—that they are making a difference.[4] As a supervisor, you will need to find ways to convey to these young employees that their work does matter.

For Gen Xers, freedom and balance are key. Gen Xers want balance in their lives. They will work hard, and in return, they will feel rewarded by time off and flexible retirement options.

Baby Boomers want recognition. Boomers want to work hard and do a good job, just like their Veteran or Traditionalist predecessors and parents, but they also want everyone to know how well they did it, whatever it is. They want the salary increase, company car, better shift, and so on—the proverbial corner office with a view. While most libraries do not provide company cars, the other examples, particularly office space and work shifts, do fit.

The expression "Hard work is its own reward" may be familiar to you, even if you heard it from a parent or grandparent rather than a coworker. For individuals in the Veteran Generation, hard work was the ultimate reward. While there are very few Veterans still in the active workforce, this belief lingers among Boomers. Libraries might want to consider part-time, flextime, or work-from-home scheduling for some Boomers, who share the need to be rewarded by being needed and valued in the workplace. Other traditional rewards, such as a coffee mug, plaque, or letter from the boss, are also appreciated by these age groups.

In addition to rewarding individuals, take care to find ways to reward group work. For groups, teams, and committees, the reward system should be tied to the group's goals and deadlines. When rewarding group members, identify the rewards that will motivate them, both individually and as a group, and then find ways to provide immediate rewards. For a team with members from multiple generations, offer a smorgasbord of rewards and let individuals choose. Rewarding the team members as they make progress, reach a milestone, or meet a deadline will motivate them to continue with the project.

For example, Jamie heads a large metadata/cataloging department in a library that recently restructured, merging the serials and monographic departments into one metadata/cataloging department. The new department is composed primarily of Baby Boomers, with 75 percent of the staff in the Baby Boomer generation, 15 percent in the Veteran Generation, 5 percent in Generation X, and 5 percent in Generation Y. Jamie himself is a Gen Xer who does not have much experience supervising Baby Boomers, although he has worked with them for several years. He wants to set up a system to recognize staff who help develop procedures that will significantly streamline workflow and free up staff to work on special projects. His library has an incentive program to reward performance on task forces and projects. Jamie decides to use the incentive program to encourage staff to look creatively at the workflow. He calls a department meeting to announce the program. He plans to award an extra vacation day to staff who propose ideas that are then implemented. His plan is met by silence. Jamie is confused. What went wrong? Why isn't his department energized by the plan? After the meeting, Jamie talks to a few of his staff individually to get their reactions. He hears from two staff members in the Baby Boom generation that they don't see any reason to reward ideas that should just be part of what good staff do. Why reward work that should be done anyway? An increase at salary time and a simple thank-you are enough of a reward. Jamie finds that his Gen X colleagues like the idea of extra vacation days. They are already dreaming up plans to overhaul the unit. The Baby Boomers are not engaged in the project. Jamie talks to a close friend in this generation, who points out that not only do the majority of the department's members expect to be included in the planning of the incentive program, but the incentives should include public recognition and acknowledgment of each person's role. Many of the Boomer-aged staff have worked at the library for many years and have plenty of vacation accrued. In fact, they feel they cannot be away from the job long enough to use what they've already accrued. Taking an extra vacation day may be pleasant for newer colleagues, but it is not a reward for many in the department.

Jamie needs to regroup. He can give the department an opportunity to modify the plan. He can include a project-end celebration and recognition

FIGURE 5.5
Different Rewards for Different Generations

Baby Boomers
- Time (errand service, dry cleaning pickup, etc.)
- Promotion and new job title
- Cash bonus
- Expensive symbolic gift (Rolex watch, etc.)
- Rewards that contribute toward plan for same standard of living at retirement
- Retirement and financial counseling

Generation X
- Challenging work
- Higher salary and better benefits
- Flexibility and freedom (work schedule)
- Daily proof that work matters
- Involvement in decision-making process
- Encouragement of flexibility and creativity
- Evidence of rewards tied directly to performance
- Clear areas of responsibility

Generation Y/Millennials/Nexters
- Meaningful work
- Learning opportunities
- Time for personal or family activities
- A fun place to work
- Autonomy
- Treated like a colleague, not a kid
- Fairness and fair play in the workplace

party along with the incentive. He can give staff a choice of two or three incentives rather than expecting everyone to want the same thing. By working with different members of the department, Jamie can create a program to recognize and reward staff in ways that will be meaningful to most staff members. Figure 5.5 presents ideas for different awards based on the generations to which employees belong.

Summary

Appropriately rewarding and recognizing staff is an important component of the overall system for encouraging top performance by your staff. Recognition programs should allow for different ways to reward staff members and should include a range of activities, from formal events to handwritten thank-you notes.

NOTES

1. Irene M. Padilla and Thomas H. Patterson, "Rewarding Employees Nonmonetarily," in *Practical Help for New Supervisors*, ed. Joan Giesecke (Chicago: American Library Association, 1997), 36–38.
2. Scott Hays, "Generation X and the Art of the Reward," *Workforce 11* (November 1999), 46; Lynne C. Lancaster and David Stillman, *When Generations Collide: Who They Are, Why They Clash; How to Solve the Generational Puzzle at Work* (New York: HarperCollins, 2002); Sue Schlichtemeier-Nutzman, presentation on multigenerational diversity for University Libraries (University of Nebraska–Lincoln, 2001).
3. Ron Zemke, Claire Raines, and Bob Filipczak, *Generations at Work: Managing the Clash of Boomers, Gen Xers, and Gen Yers in Your Workplace* (New York: AMACOM, 2013).
4. Susanna Kultalahti and Riitta Viitala, "Generation Y: Challenging Clients for HRM?," *Journal of Managerial Psychology* 30, no. 1 (2015): 101–14; Crystal Hoole and Jackie Bonnema, "Work Engagement and Meaningful Work across Generational Cohorts," *The SA Journal of Human Resource Management* 13, no. 1 (2015), 11 pages, doi: 10.4102/sajhrm.v13i1.681.

PART TWO

Managing Groups

Becoming a Manager

Chris has just started work as a department head at the local university. She was recruited from another state institution and is looking forward to working at the university. Chris has lots of questions about the unit and is just getting started when there is a knock on her door. Phil, an experienced member of the department, enters. Chris smiles hello. Phil begins and explains how he should have gotten the job as the senior member of the department. Phil leaves Chris feeling a bit confused. Other members stop in to introduce themselves and to wish her luck. Looking at the disarray in the office, Chris figures she will need all the luck she can get.

Jamie has started work as the head of another department the same day Chris joined the reference department. Jamie has been with the library for four years and was promoted from within the department. On his first day, staff drop by to congratulate Jamie and to voice concerns. Bottlenecks have been occurring between cataloging and acquisitions, and the head of acquisitions wants to know what Jamie is going to do to solve this problem. Another colleague drops in to repeat her long-standing concern about having an adjustable chair for her desk. What is Jamie going to do about this?

By the end of the day, both Chris and Jamie have a pretty good idea of just exactly what they have gotten into. Both thought supervisor positions would give them more time to look at policies and help implement a vision for the unit. Instead, they each spent the day on small details that others should have been able to handle. How will they each turn around their units to make them functional, productive parts of the operation? Welcome to the world of supervision and management.

If the above day sounds intriguing, you are thinking like a manager. Chris and Jamie are quickly discovering that management is not about technical skills. Rather, it is about helping to solve problems, developing staff, and creating a positive working environment. Chris and Jamie have their work cut out for them. Each must change his or her own perspective, learn to see the unit differently, and learn how the job has now changed. They could use some training, advice, and help.

Let's explore what it takes to be a supervisor, head, or manager of a unit, department, or organization.

Competencies

What are the core competencies for today's supervisors and managers? What skills, knowledge, and personal attributes will contribute to your success as a manager? If you think that the ability to give commands and control your unit will make you successful, you will be disappointed. Today, when leading groups, supervisors and managers must move beyond the command and control mentality to develop skills in coaching, facilitation, and negotiation. You will need to be customer and community focused, able to support and implement change in response to the changing information environment, and able to work in or lead teams and groups, while ensuring that your unit is productive and meets organizational goals and objectives.

Supervisory or managerial competencies can be divided into a number of groups.[1] Key skills that are the foundation for any position include technical or functional competence, communication skills, time management skills, and cultural competence. In addition, supervisors, managers, and other members of the organization must demonstrate flexibility and exhibit self-awareness.

Next, supervisors need to have good problem-solving and decision-making skills and be effective at building teams and managing conflict. Supervisors need to demonstrate personnel management skills, including coaching and developing staff, setting standards and expectations, and conducting performance reviews.

As one advances in management, planning and budgeting skills become more important. Negotiating among and across units or departments also becomes a part of one's role. Finally, thinking about the organization as a whole and working to develop and achieve organizational goals round out a manager's role.

Managers must demonstrate these competencies themselves and be responsible for coaching staff to help them develop these important competencies.

Myths versus Reality

Besides building new competencies, supervisors need to let go of a number of myths about management that no longer apply to today's workplace.[2]

Myth: You are in charge of everything. *Reality*: If you think about this statement, you will realize that you cannot be in charge of every detail in your unit. Staff continually make decisions about their tasks, procedures, and work. If they did not make decisions, they would not be doing their jobs. As a manager, you are responsible for setting the overall direction and seeing that the work is done, and while you want to be sure you pitch in and help when needed, you are not doing your staff any favors if you try to do their work in addition to your own. Managers must delegate for the success of their units.

Myth: You cannot trust your staff. *Reality*: This myth assumes that staff are not going to do their jobs well and that management must spend time preventing poor performance. This attitude is not helpful in today's workplace, where building motivated teams of staff who take pride in their work is an important part of creating a productive, positive environment. If you do not trust your staff, ask yourself why you hired them and why you are retaining them. Instead of assuming the worst and preparing to act on it, assume you have talented staff and provide appropriate training and direction and trust them to do their best work.

Myth: You cannot show emotion as a manager. *Reality*: Although management theorists in the 1970s advised that managers should not show emotion, today's successful manager knows that managing emotions, or emotional intelligence, is an important part of her responsibilities. Emotional intelligence includes the two core components of "the ability to manage one's own emotions and the ability to understand and recognize the emotions of others."[3] By managing his or her own emotions, a manager can establish a positive working environment that centers on respect for all. By recognizing the emotions of others, a manager can adjust his or her style and reactions to limit negativity and promote a constructive response to a given situation.

Myth: You must always defend your staff. *Reality*: Perhaps one of the hardest things to learn as a new manager is that you need to support your staff and still recognize when performance issues have to be addressed. For example, if Chris hears from her boss that library users are complaining about the poor treatment they receive at the desk, then Chris needs to investigate the complaints and work to improve the service in the department rather than spend time defending her staff to her boss without knowing if the complaints are valid or not.

Myth: You always have to be right. *Reality*: As a manager, you need to learn to admit when you made a mistake and take action to correct the problem. If you assume you must always be right, then you may ignore information that runs counter to your own beliefs. You also need to learn when to compromise and back down from a position that is no longer valid. Learning to see the big picture and recognizing when you can learn from others is an important part of being a manager.

Roles

Letting go of these traditional and dated ideas about management will help you, as a manager, be open to taking on new roles and approaches to managing your unit. As a manager and supervisor, you will communicate vision and set direction and will have a number of new roles.[4] These roles include the following:

- Mentor to your staff
- Facilitator for managing conflict
- Monitor of your unit's performance
- Coordinator of projects
- Planner for your unit
- Creator working productively with your staff
- Broker and negotiator for your unit
- Innovator for managing change

Management Style

To carry out these roles, Chris and Jamie will need to develop an appropriate management style. At first, Jamie may think that success will come as long as everyone likes him, as they did when he was a colleague. All he needs to do is keep people happy. But if Jamie follows this path, he will soon find that happy staff are not necessarily productive staff. Chris may think that the same skills that make a good parent make a good supervisor. But treating her staff as one would treat children also will not be effective. The workplace is populated with adults, and Chris needs to treat her staff as adults.

Management styles can be described in terms of staff concern and task concern.[5] A manager who is concerned with tasks but not concerned with people will be very autocratic. This command and control approach, common in the early twentieth century, was a one-way process in which decisions were made by the manager and staff needs were ignored. While minimal work got done, the environment did not foster excellence. New to the organization, Chris may quickly see problems and be tempted to act on them and make changes without taking time to get to know the staff. Today's staff are more likely to rebel and leave rather than stay in a stifling work environment.

A manager who is concerned about staff but not tasks is out to win a popularity contest. This manager makes decisions to make people happy. Conflicts are smoothed over rather than resolved. While staff may be happy, they are not likely to be challenged to do their best. As an internal promotion, Jamie may struggle with this.

A manager who avoids both task and people issues basically abdicates any responsibility for the unit. Here there is little or no communication, conflict is avoided, and only safe decisions are made. The absentee manager leaves the unit to fend for itself, and the unit may begin to feel disconnected from the rest of the larger organization.

Finally, the manager who is concerned about people and productivity will seek to create an environment that encourages people to do their best. Communication is two-way, conflicts are resolved, and staff are encouraged to grow and develop, contribute ideas, and share in planning. These managers are most likely to create a positive working environment.

To be effective, Chris and Jamie need to develop styles that balance concern for tasks with concern for people. When they can balance these two elements, they will be more likely to succeed.

As Chris and Jamie finish their first days, they may find their lists of roles, skills, and abilities overwhelming. How can Chris and Jamie begin to establish themselves as supervisors even as they work to develop other skills needed to do their jobs?

The Manager's View

One of the things that Jamie has to learn as a manager who was promoted from within is that his view or perspective on the organization needs to change. He is no longer one of the staff members. He needs to have an understanding of the whole unit and how his unit fits into the organization. He needs to develop relations with other supervisors, with his staff, and with his boss.

Chris and Jamie will find that a manager's job is filled with ambiguity. A successful manager will learn to expect the unexpected. Facing multiple, unrelated issues and problems ranging from the insignificant to the important is part of a typical manager's day. Chris and Jamie will find that a manager's job is no longer about being a producer of services. Nor will either of them be an expert for a particular service or task. Rather, they will find that they need to know a little about a lot of tasks and have a solid understanding of how the work of their units fits into the larger organization. Breadth replaces depth of knowledge. Therefore, Chris and Jamie must learn to rely on staff to be the experts. They will need to trust staff to know the intricacies of each task, while they themselves will need to understand how all the tasks fit together. They will come to see that management is a position of interdependence, because managers need to guide their staff to excel even as they depend on them to make the unit a success.[6]

Many new managers may be surprised at how their views must change if they are to be successful. As Chris and Jamie set direction, solve problems, and handle daily crises, they need to get to know their respective staff from the perspective of a supervisor. Whether you are promoted from within or hired from outside the library, as a new supervisor, it is important to get to know each staff member as an individual. In the first few weeks on the job, you should set aside time to meet with each staff member to learn about his or her job and listen to his or her concerns. This is not the time to do most of the talking in order to establish yourself as the boss, but instead to listen. This is a supervisor's best opportunity to establish a new working relationship with each member of the unit. In these conversations, ask open-ended questions about each person's job. This will help encourage staff to share their ideas and concerns. You can find out what people like about their jobs, what things are challenging to them, and what things they might like to see changed. You will want to keep the conversation friendly and work related. This is not an informal, social conversation. It is an important, work-related conversation that will help you, as a supervisor, begin to understand the intricacies and complexities of the unit. It is also important to ask each person the same question to start the conversation. Sending out two or three questions ahead of the meeting will give staff a chance to think about what they want to say. Using the same questions as a starting point will assure staff that they are all being treated in a similar manner. Even though each conversation will be different, starting out in a similar way will let staff control what other types of information they want to share initially.

Building a Relationship with Your Supervisor

Chris and Jamie also need to have a series of conversations with their respective bosses in order to learn how they fit into the overall organization. As a manager, Chris may be part of an overall public services division. She will want to find out how her unit's work impacts the work of other units in the division. For example, if interlibrary loan is part of the circulation unit but the reference desk answers questions for interlibrary loan materials, then Chris will want to confirm what the expectations are for her unit regarding interlibrary loan material. Chris and Jamie will also want to clarify performance expectations with their bosses. To continue the previous example,

Chris needs to know how quickly interlibrary loan requests are filled so her unit can give accurate information to patrons about the service. Clarifying expectations in the beginning will help Chris set a positive tone for working with her boss.

In establishing a working relationship with your new boss, think about the kind of employee you want working for you and determine how you can be that same type of employee for your boss. Key characteristics of a productive employer-employee relationship include those discussed in the following paragraphs.[7]

Supportive. Look for ways to support your boss, your organization, and your organization's policies and procedures. Think about what you can do to ensure that policies are implemented in your unit and that your unit is contributing to organization goals.

Positive. Bring a positive and respectful attitude to work. While your boss is not always right, nor would you want to follow him or her blindly, you will want to begin with the assumption that the boss knows what he or she is doing. A positive attitude also includes watching your own moods. Although we are not likely to be cheerful every day, it is important to not pout about every little mishap. An even-tempered approach to the workplace will go a long way to creating a positive, productive environment and a good working relationship with your boss.

Good work habits. You set the tone for your unit. When you arrive on time, do not take excessively long breaks, and keep a neat work area, you send a signal that you care about your job. This message is important for both your supervisor and your staff.

Willingness to learn. In today's changing information environment, it is crucial that we are always ready and willing to learn new things. Look for ways to increase knowledge of your job, your unit, and your organization. You can help your unit stay up-to-date in this changing field while showing your boss that you care about improving your unit.

On-time completion of assigned work. While you spend a lot of time as a supervisor building relationships and interacting with your staff, it is also important to make sure that assigned tasks are completed. When your boss asks for a report or paperwork is due, get it done on time.

Working well with others. Your boss will look to you to build good working relationships with other supervisors in the department and in the organization. Look for ways to build networks and avoid the "us versus them" syndrome.

Building a Working Relationship with Your Peers

Chris and Jamie also need to begin building working relationships with their peers. Their peers are other supervisors in their units and in the organization. This is their new group of colleagues. If they see their peers as competitors, they will find it difficult to build supportive relationships. They may see the actions of other units as threats to their own groups. They may become defensive around other managers. Such an approach will likely lead to conflict and failure.

As a supervisor new to the library, Chris will soon learn that her peers are her main support group. Other supervisors can provide advice on how to handle problems, how the organization functions, and how to succeed in the organization. They can help Chris see things from a different perspective and help her formulate plans.

Chris and Jamie may also find it useful to get to know each other as new supervisors and to compare experiences. When you are new to any organization, it can be very helpful to talk to other new people to learn about their efforts within the institution or organization. New managers may be willing to talk more openly among themselves in a group that will not be evaluating their work as closely as a boss or members of their own departments. Working together, new managers can also divide the time it takes to get answers to common questions and to share these answers with the group. By dividing up orientation tasks among themselves, supervisors can benefit from one another's expertise as they learn about the organization.

Unfortunately, some colleagues will not be interested in creating a positive working environment. They may be disillusioned, long-term employees who resist change. Chris and Jamie will need to recognize this negative behavior and avoid letting someone else's negative view of the organization influence their attitudes. Chris and Jamie cannot change these people, but they can take steps to prevent them from spreading their negative views in their units.

As a supervisor promoted from within, Jamie will need to develop a new relationship with other managers. He may have to remind some people, through his words and actions, that he is a manager now. He can also benefit from having face-to-face meetings with his new peers to find out how their units work and how they can develop new partnerships.

As Chris and Jamie develop good working relationships with their peers and build a lateral team in the organization, they will be better able to expand their views of the organization and to work to integrate their unit into the department or institution.

Learning the Job

While you are building working relationships with your staff, your boss, and your peers, you will also be learning the tasks that are part of your job. You are an expert in some areas, which is why you have the new job, but you still need to learn these tasks from a manager's view. You will want to understand and learn all the details you may have missed as an employee or staff member. Now is the time to learn from your predecessor and your colleagues.

Your Predecessor

If you can meet with your predecessor, you may find that you can gather valuable information about your unit. Your predecessor can provide a unique view of the unit as well as insights into why the unit functions as it does. However, you will want to examine the information critically. You were hired to help the unit grow and improve. You will want to establish your own approach and style. Nonetheless, the information you receive can be useful if interpreted with careful judgment.

You may be facing a situation where you were brought in to make changes because your predecessor was not successful. In such a case, you may still want to meet with your predecessor, but you should recognize that the person may not be very objective about the organization.

If you can meet with your predecessor, plan the conversation to get to the information that will be most helpful to you. Subjects to raise include the following:

> *Department structure.* Ask what works and what does not work about the current structure.
>
> *Mission and goals.* Learn about your predecessor's view of the unit's mission and goals. How well is the unit meeting its goals?
>
> *Personnel strengths and challenges.* Find out what personnel issues you will need to address. Learn how your predecessor views the staff. Then remember that you will want to make your own assessment.

Budget. Learn how the budget was developed. What is included and what is missing? What resources are needed for the unit?

Committee assignments. Are there particular committee meetings you should attend? How are decisions made? What is your likely role?

Hidden problems. Can your predecessor alert you to hidden land mines in the unit? What pitfalls do you need to avoid?[8]

The information you gather in this conversation can be a helpful guide. Remember, though, to weigh the information you get against other information you gather as you meet with your staff and colleagues. Your predecessor's input can be invaluable, but it is from one perspective and just one of the sources of information you will collect.

Office Files

Another important source of information about the unit or department is the unit's operations manuals and files. These files may be online, and it is important to find out how to access electronic files and who can access these records or documents. From the written documentation, you will learn how tasks are supposed to be done. You can find out about policies and procedures, paperwork, and forms. While you will find that there are some variations in how tasks are actually done, the manuals will help you learn how the tasks should be done.

Reports. Annual reports, committee minutes, and task force reports are also a rich source of information. These historical documents will help you understand the origin and development of your unit. You will also learn what problems have been solved and which ones keep reappearing. If you cannot find reports for your unit, ask your staff if they have copies you could borrow. Check to see if your organization has an archive of historical documents and see if you can find unit reports there. Usually, someone will have copies of some of the reports you need. Do ask others for help in finding these documents.

Personnel files. The official personnel files will give you background information on each member of your unit. You will also see how staff have been evaluated, what problems have been addressed, and what successes have been celebrated. You may find it more effective to talk to each staff member first and begin to form your own judgments before reading past performance reviews. You will want to make sure you are being open and objective as you begin to learn about your staff. You will want to watch that you are not unduly influenced by your predecessor's view of the staff.

By reviewing the documentation available about your unit, you will learn how tasks are done, how policies and procedures are carried out, and how the unit documentation is created and saved. All this information will help you learn your job as you learn about the group you now manage.

Summary

At the end of their first days, each of our new supervisors sits down to take stock. Chris handled user complaints, found out the budget was only slightly out of balance, and wondered what to do about the student who was not showing up for work. Chris realized that no one was going to create an orientation schedule for her or tell her how to do her job. Instead, Chris created her first major "to do" list and thought about how she should proceed with her job. Her list included a schedule for the next few months. On her list, Chris put the following:

Hold a brief fifteen-minute meeting each morning with staff to review the work for the day, as a way to decrease the number of unexpected crises and events.

Schedule individual meetings with staff members. Do two per day.

Set aside one to two hours each day to read files, documents, and reports.

Schedule a meeting with her boss.

Schedule meetings with other supervisors. Try for one or two a week.

Review department goals and objectives and assess progress each month.

Jamie's day was similar. He reassured a staff member who was upset about potential changes in workflow. He met with a few of his librarians and learned that their opinions on issues were very diverse. Jamie realized that learning to collaborate and work more as a team will be a key to the unit's success. Jamie also decided to have coffee with Chris soon to compare notes as new supervisors. Jamie's "to do" list included these items:

Schedule thirty-minute meetings with each librarian and staff member in the unit.

Schedule twenty minutes each day, at a minimum, to read reports.

Schedule a meeting with his supervisor.

Meet with Chris for coffee and to debrief.

By developing plans for learning about their units and their jobs, Chris and Jamie will be better able to manage their units even as they learn how to be managers.

NOTES

1. Elizabeth Fuseler Avery, Terry Dahlin, and Deborah Carver, *Staff Development: A Practical Guide*, 3rd ed. (Chicago: American Library Association, 2001).

2. Morey Stettner, *Skills for New Managers* (New York: McGraw-Hill, 2000), 15–27.

3. Peter Hernon, Joan Giesecke, and Camila Alire, *Academic Librarians as Emotionally Intelligent Leaders* (Westport, CT: Libraries Unlimited, 2008), 2.

4. Avery, Dahlin, and Carver, *Staff Development*, 65.

5. Robert Lefton and Jerome Loeb, *Why Can't We Get Anything Done around Here?* (New York: McGraw-Hill, 2004), 100–121.

6. Linda Hill, *Becoming a Manager* (Boston: Harvard Business School Press, 2003), 52.

7. Martin Broadwell and Carol Broadwell Dietrich, *The New Supervisor: How to Thrive in Your First Year as a Manager* (Cambridge, MA: Perseus Books, 1998), 27–29.

8. Edward Betof and Frederic Harwood, *Just Promoted! How to Survive and Thrive in Your First 12 Months as a Manager* (New York: McGraw-Hill, 1992), 22–23.

7

Teamwork and Group Dynamics

Managing teams is part of the new challenge for today's managers. Interdivisional teams, horizontal work groups, and a variety of collaborative arrangements are replacing many of the traditional functional and hierarchical structures in our organizations. Managers today must manage interdependent groups and create a culture of cooperation in the midst of older management structures that emphasize and reward individual effort over group effort. How can managers bring these opposing processes together to create effective working groups?

Definition of Team

One of the first problems in determining how to manage groups is to figure out what type of working group or team environment exists or is desired in the organization. The term *team* is used to describe everything from tightly knit, interdependent working groups to loosely structured gatherings of individuals who barely work together. *Team* can refer to a unit or department, a group of managers, a two-person pairing such as a partnership, or the whole organization. Sometimes it seems that organizations have created teams simply by taking the departmental structure and renaming the departments as teams without making any changes in how the group functions or is managed.

Even in sports, it is difficult to identify a single type of team. For example, a football team is a highly structured group with defined roles. Players come to one another's aid only as prescribed by the structure and rules of the game. That is, the quarterback of the football team is not going to be on the field with the defense no matter how badly the defense is playing. Nonetheless, the group plays as a team, with individual roles subordinate to the team as a whole. Contrast this tightly knit, hierarchical approach to a golf team where individual performance is most important and there is little interdependence among the players. Baseball teams fall somewhere between these two types of teams, with players functioning independently in their individual positions but needing to interact in prescribed ways on the field if they are to win the game. In organizations, the independent golf team approach of each person doing his or her own job with little interaction with others is becoming obsolete. Rather, organizations are finding that teams or work groups that require collaboration, commitment, and trust are more common and more productive than independent groups. But given this wide range of types of teams, what does the term really mean in the workplace?

Jon Katzenbach and Douglas Smith, in their book *The Wisdom of Teams*, provide a succinct definition of a team. They describe a true working team as "a small number of people with complementary skills who are committed to a common purpose, performance goals, and approach for which they hold themselves mutually accountable."[1] The key concepts in this definition help define the requirements for a true working team. To be a team, the group needs to be small enough so that people can interact regularly and effectively. Team members get to know one another, build working relationships, and meet regularly. When the group gets too big, often more than twenty-five people, it becomes more difficult to meet, to interact, and to work together. In larger groups, subgroups may form and the whole unit no longer functions as a coordinated team. Rather, the larger group may follow team values but not have the interactions that characterize effective teams.

Team members possess complementary skills rather than identical skills. Each team member brings unique skills to the group so that the group as a whole has all the proficiencies needed to accomplish assigned tasks. Having a group of people all with the same skills doing the same task is a working unit rather than a team. A group of online cataloging staff who all do the same task of cataloging materials using records on OCLC is a working unit, not a team. Each person's performance is independent of the others in the group. While group goals can be developed in a working unit, the individual employees can set their own pace and can do much of their work without consulting others as long as standards and expectations are clear. Here team values may be useful, but the group is not a true team.

The overall picture for a team is an interdependent group with a common goal or purpose. The team members are working toward and accept an agreed-upon purpose or set of goals. Individuals do not set their own goals. Rather, group goals define the course for the team. In football, for example, the defense may have team goals on how many turnovers they want to cause in a game. In the library, the interlibrary loan staff may create goals focused on the turn-around time and fill rate for requests. To achieve these goals, the group members must work together. Goals cannot be achieved by individual effort alone.

Team members also agree on how the work will be done. Internal procedures are explored and agreed to by the team. Problem-solving and decision-making processes are clear and understood by all members of the team. Team members also understand that each person contributes to the work of the whole. The amount of work that is done is equitably distributed, with each team member contributing to the best of his or her ability. Unlike groups where some people may contribute very little but get credit for the work of the whole, in a true team, all team members agree to participate to make the team a success.

This brings us to shared accountability, a key factor in a true team. Team members agree to take responsibility for their own work and the work of the team. They help out one another as needed. They encourage one another to do the best that each member can do for the team. Individual responsibility gives way to group responsibility, mutual respect, and support.

Characteristics of Effective Teams

If the group you are managing fits the definition of a true team, then your next step as a manager is to understand the characteristics of an effective team, because not all teams function well. Teams can be as dysfunctional as any unit or department regardless of management style. Successful teams, though, have the following characteristics:

> Team members understand and support the organization's vision and goals.
>
> Teams share a set of values about quality service.
>
> Teams work to improve work processes and operations.
>
> Team members discuss and agree as to how decisions will be made, how communication will occur, and how the group will be managed.
>
> Team members listen to one another, respect one another, and trust one another.
>
> Assignments and responsibilities are clear. Roles are clear and understood.
>
> Teams effectively manage external policies, processes, and politics.
>
> Teams set results-oriented goals.
>
> Teamwork enhances the ability of the team members to work together; that is, team members continue to learn how to work together more effectively. Team members are satisfied to work together.
>
> Team members adapt to changing environments, anticipate one another's moves, and learn to regenerate themselves as they work together.
>
> Successful teams have committed, focused leaders who facilitate group success.[2]

Glenn Parker, in *Team Players and Teamwork*, describes twelve characteristics of effective teams.[3] His list is similar to the previous one. Parker includes clear purpose, informality within the team, participation, effective listening skills, civil disagreement, consensus decision making, open communication, clear roles, shared leadership, effective external relations, style diversity, and self-assessment as core characteristics of teams. As you review these characteristics of teams, as team leader, you will likely find that when the team members practice effective listening skills and open communication, the team will function as a coherent group.

Teamwork, then, can be described as a "frame of mind, a belief, and a commitment, not just a program."[4] In a team, group goals are more important than individual goals. Team members believe in the value of group processes and work to ensure that processes complement productivity. In other words, decision-making systems, communication systems, and work processes are equally important to meeting the team's goals. Productivity is not sacrificed to ensure good group interactions, nor are good group interaction skills ignored in order to maintain or improve productivity. A cohesive approach that brings team values together with team productivity is crucial if one is to create a true team.

How Can You Recognize a True Team?

An example from an interlibrary loan unit might illustrate some of the differences between a work group and a team. Imagine an interlibrary loan unit with five staff members and one supervisor. Two staff members work on lending requests, two work on borrowing requests, and one serves as a reception desk attendant. A problem arises with the workflow between a branch library and the main library for obtaining books requested by other libraries in a timely manner. In a work group, the lending staff might discuss the problem with the unit supervisor and generate possible solutions. The unit supervisor might set up a meeting with branch and interlibrary loan staff. Then the group discusses the problem and proposes solutions. The supervisor decides which solution to implement. While the various staff involved provide input and discuss the issues, they are not empowered to make a decision and implement that decision.

In a team environment, the five interlibrary loan staff and the supervisor would discuss the problem with the branch staff. The group as a whole would generate options, assess possibilities, and decide the best way to improve workflow to meet agreed-upon goals for turnaround time. Lending and borrowing staff would participate in the discussion because changes in work routines could potentially impact the unit in any number of ways.

By working together, the unit and branch staff will likely find solutions that work for all units involved. The group is not only responsible for implementing the changes but also accountable for their success.

Agreed-upon goals, responsibility, and shared accountability are all part of a true team environment. This still leaves the question of how to recognize a true team. What distinguishes a team from a working group? Again, we can turn to Katzenbach and Smith, who created a performance curve for teams and groups to illustrate the differences among types of working groups. They use performance impact and team effectiveness to distinguish between types of work groups.[5] At one end of the scale are working groups. Working groups are probably the most common form of structure in our organizations. In these units, individual effort is the primary measurement for unit success. Members may come together to share information, insights, or ideas on how to improve the unit. However, individual performance goals are more important than joint work products. Members of the unit interact but are not dependent on one another for either their own or the unit's success.

The second type of unit can be described as a pseudoteam. Here the work of the unit lends itself to true group-based performance, but the members of the unit do not and are not interested in working together to achieve unit-wide goals. These units are not very productive because individual interests are more important to members than group success. Pseudoteams may form when a manager or library director decides to rename work units as teams without making any changes in group interactions. The label for the group changes without any change in how the group functions.

The next type of group on the performance continuum is the potential team. Potential teams are those groups that are trying to improve group performance, are becoming committed to group goals, and are beginning to recognize the need for mutual respect and accountability. If you are a manager with a potential team, you can help the group achieve high productivity through team development and training. Potential teams in an organization offer managers the chance to implement change and achieve success.

Real teams, the next group on the continuum, are those units that meet the definition of a team and are reaching mutually agreed-upon goals. These groups are effective, productive, and can be successful over time.

High-performance teams are at the end of the continuum. These groups not only function effectively but also are deeply committed to one another's growth and success. These teams surpass goals, have high energy levels, and

FIGURE 7.1

Team Performance Characteristics

TYPE OF GROUP	MOTIVATION TO PERFORM	MEASURES OF TEAM SUCCESS
Work group	Individual goals	Successful or not successful
Pseudoteam	Selfish interests	Not successful
Potential team	Organization sets group goals	Partially successful
Real team	Mutually agreed-upon goals	Successful
High-performance team	Surpasses goals, committed to team growth	Most successful

provide support for one another while meeting organizational goals. The performance characteristics of these five types of groups are summarized in figure 7.1.

As a supervisor or team leader in a team-based organization, you will want to move your group from a potential team to a real or a high-performance team. If you have a work group, then a team structure may not be the best way to organize your unit. Here you need to look at the purpose and organizational goals for your unit. If interdependence is not a key factor in accomplishing your goals, then a team structure may not be needed. A solid working group that shares team values and meets its performance goals may be most effective for your unit. If you have a pseudoteam, you will need to do a lot of staff development and training to change your unit from a group to a team.

Developing Teams

Before you begin a team-building program, it is helpful to look at the context in which your unit operates because the context impacts team effectiveness. James Shonk, in his book *Working in Teams*, outlines five factors that impact teams: environmental influences, goals, roles, processes, and relationships.[6] Let's look at each of these factors as they apply to our interlibrary loan unit.

Environmental influences. Environmental influences are the external forces that impact teamwork. These include such things as policies, reward systems, organization structures, customers, and governmental regulations. For the interlibrary loan unit, organizational policies such as who can use the service, how the service is funded, and what hours the library is open will frame how the unit functions. Reward structures for how salaries are distributed or what types of awards are available can also impact the unit. For example, if only individual effort is rewarded, it will be more difficult to convince the staff to work as a team. Lending operations staff may be less inclined to support borrowing staff if the former's efforts are not acknowledged by the organization.

Goals. Agreed-upon goals are the foundation for teamwork. Goals need to be clear, specific, and shared. In interlibrary loan, goals focused on turnaround time, fill rate, and quantity of work to be accomplished all determine how the group will design the workflow. For example, if a goal of a twenty-four-hour turnaround time on lending requests is set and lending staff have an unusually busy day, then in a team approach, borrowing staff would help the lending staff complete their work. The team as a whole takes responsibility for achieving the goal.

Roles. Clarifying roles means deciding who does what. For interlibrary loan, for example, the group needs to know who processes lending requests, who monitors OCLC requests, who oversees mail operations, and who manages the reception desk. It is also important for the group to know who the primary backup is for each task and how team members will know when their help is needed.

Processes. The term *processes* refers to the internal procedures that determine how the team does its work. In interlibrary loan, the team decides how long to spend on difficult requests before referring them to someone else. The team also needs to decide how decisions will be made and how meetings will be run. The team members decide and agree to which libraries will be contacted for materials and in what order, how consortium arrangements impact lending response and borrowing options, and how materials will be delivered to patrons. All these processes should be clear to all members of the team.

Relationships. The last factor to consider in understanding your team is the quality of the interpersonal interactions. Team members should develop their own guidelines on how they will interact, how difficult issues will be discussed, and how disagreements will be handled. In interlibrary loan, disagreements about what steps to take to resolve a customer problem need to be addressed. Staff must develop ways to express and address different opinions and viewpoints. If they do not address these issues, team effectiveness will suffer.

To summarize, these five factors are key considerations as you design team-building programs for your team. Addressing these areas in your development program will help improve team effectiveness.

Designing the Team-Building Program

Team-building programs can vary from a short discussion on the value of teams to a multiday retreat with a trained facilitator. How you design your team-building program will depend on how your organization functions and how the organization supports staff development. Does your organization have a formal staff development program or training unit? Does the organization have funds you can use to hire a facilitator to help? Does the organization have trained facilitators you can consult as you think about staff development? Know what resources you can use and what support you can find before you decide on a particular program or approach.

No matter how you design staff development efforts for team building, there are some common guidelines for success that you can follow,[7] which are described in more detail in the remainder of this section.

Establish clear goals. Be specific about what you want your team building to accomplish. Do you need new goals, new standards, or a new structure? Clarifying your goals will help guide your planning and lead to a successful assessment process at the end.

Get input. Effective team building starts by getting team members to help design the program. Involving team members in the planning will help get buy-in for the program. Imposing a training program on the group will be less effective.

Model constructive behavior. Focus on behavior and performance in the training rather than on judging opinions or positions. Staff should learn the effects that different behaviors have on the unit and how appropriate behaviors can improve team performance.

Stay work oriented. It is important to avoid team building that can become too emotional, with too much sharing of non-work-related information. Stay focused on projects and the responsibilities of the team. In interlibrary loan, for example, training examples should be based on the processes of borrowing and lending materials and on document delivery rather than on the personal lives of the team members.

Allow time for change. Team building takes time. Change can happen, but it will not happen overnight. Team members need time to practice new skills, try new processes, and explore new ideas. Look for incremental progress and reward even small positive changes.

Assess development. Teams can conduct self-assessments throughout the development and training process so that the team can judge its own progress. Have the team members individually complete assessment tools and then discuss the results. Team members can use these discussions as opportunities to plan and guide future development efforts.

Assessment tools usually ask team members to rank how well the team is doing in the following areas:

- Clarifying purpose
- Clarifying expectations
- Developing open communication systems
- Providing mutual support
- Developing conflict resolution skills
- Clarifying decision-making processes
- Encouraging risk taking
- Sharing leadership
- Sharing feedback[8]

Develop realistic expectations. Credibility and trust are easy to lose if you set expectations that cannot be met by the group. Expectations for training should address those factors that are within the group's control. For example, increasing understanding of each person's role, clarifying team goals, and improving conflict-resolution skills are all factors that the team can control. Training in these areas will result in team improvement.

Utilize outside consultants. Finally, if possible, it can be very helpful to engage an outside trainer or facilitator to assist with team development. An outside person can help facilitate communication and remain objective more easily than someone from inside the team. Bringing in an outside person can help the team see new approaches and find new ways of working together.

Following these concepts will help you design effective training for your group no matter what training methods are used.

Team Training Plans

There are many ways to develop training plans and many methods that can be used. As a manager, you will want to match the training method to your team's needs and your organization's culture.

Describing all the possible training options is beyond the scope of this work. You can find helpful examples of training methods in the third edition of *Staff Development: A Practical Guide*, by Elizabeth Fuseler Avery, Terry Dahlin, and Deborah Carver.[9] In their book *Just Promoted!*, Edward Betof and Frederic Harwood include a matrix you can use to evaluate the type of training that is needed and the methods that will be most successful.[10] In *Learn Library Management*, by Bob Pymm and Damon Hickey, you will find two exercises and a case study that will help you build effective teams.[11] Designing good training programs takes time, thought, and resources. Your organization's staff development experts can be very helpful to you as you develop programs to build and strengthen your team.

When Teams Fail

What causes teams to fail? Why don't all work groups succeed as teams? The causes for failure are numerous because teams are often a paradox. Team leaders and teams balance

- individual differences and collective identity,
- support with confrontation, and
- management authority with team autonomy.[12]

These conflicting ideas and concepts must be brought into harmony for teams to succeed.

Numerous forces are working against team success in the organization. Some of these forces include lack of respect, selfishness, politics, blame, and decision-making dilemmas.[13] Immature approaches to the team by individual team members can defeat even the best team-building efforts.

Lack of respect. If team members do not have respect for one another or for the organization, it will be difficult, if not impossible, to turn the group into a team. It may be more productive to move people out of the group and get new members in order to build a viable team.

Selfishness. When staff members care more about what they can get as individuals than they do about the group, you will have problems building a team. Staff who argue over who gets a new standing desk or preferred desk shift are not ready for team building. Here, as a supervisor and manager, you need to step back and start with basic training in good group skills before you can begin team building.

Politics. If organizational politics are more important than the team, you have an immature group. Again, look for training options on basic skills to help staff move beyond an individual focus to thinking about group goals.

Blame. If the group starts the conversation about a problem with "who is to blame," you have an immature group. An interlibrary loan staff, for example, that blames others for poor turnaround time instead of looking for a solution they can implement is not a well-functioning team. Blaming poor shelving, branch staff ineptitude, or poorly documented user requests are all examples of immature group behavior.

Decision-making dilemmas. Another area where teams can experience difficulty is in decision making. Team leaders may find that team members spend an excessive amount of time discussing choices but then are unwilling to reach a decision. This process leaves the team leader making the decisions. Bob Frisch refers to this process as the dictator-by-default syndrome, explaining that the problem arises because team members are trying to reach consensus but are using their individual preferences in the discussions.[14] Frisch notes that three or more people trying to choose among more than three options will generate conflicting majorities for all of the possibilities. Thus, an impasse forms and the team leader is forced to make a decision, and that decision will satisfy only a small portion of the team.[15] To avoid the decision-making dilemma, Frisch advises teams to use different tactics, such as evaluating the pros and cons of various options in order to keep the discussion more open on the possible options; examining assumptions about the options in order to be sure options are not being prematurely eliminated; brainstorming activities that are focused on real possibilities and that avoid nonsense options; and devising new options that combine the best features of existing options.[16] These strategies help the team have an open discussion of options in order to reach better decisions.

In all these cases, the culture of the group or the group members need to change before true team building can begin.

Manager's Role in Teams

By now you may be wondering what your role as a manager is in the team environment. Are you a team leader, a team member, or just one of the crowd? What role do you play in this type of organizational structure? As team leader, you are responsible for the following tasks.[17]

Understand and be committed to the team concept. First, as a manager, you need to understand the team concept. If you play favorites or reward and promote individual achievement over group goals, you will undermine team efforts. If you are not committed to a team structure, you will not be effective as a team leader.

Select team members. As team leader, you are responsible for choosing the members of your team. Look for complementary skills so you can build a group of people with the variety and depth of skills you need for success. Research shows that diverse groups are more successful at seeing problems from a variety of perspectives and are more successful at solving them.[18]

Develop people skills. As a manager, you need to recognize and acknowledge team members' skill-building efforts. Even something as simple as saying, "Good job" or "That's a good effort" will support people-building skills. Recognizing that different people want different types of recognition is important too. Some people like public recognition; others prefer a personal letter. As a team leader, you need to understand your team members as individuals while also promoting group coordination and collaboration. Being responsive to and supportive of team members will help maximize individual performance and contribute to team success.

Facilitate information flow. Another major role for you as leader is to facilitate, support, and promote the flow of information. You bring in information from the rest of the organization. You facilitate the sharing of information about your unit with the organization. And you support the coordination of effort within the group through the sharing of information. As team leader, you are responsible for encouraging quieter team members to participate and to express their opinions while working with more forceful members to learn to listen to their colleagues.

Coordinate with your peers. As team leader, you are charged with working effectively with other team leaders to advance the goals of the organization. In interlibrary loan, for example, you may be working with an acquisition unit to be sure that heavily requested items are considered for purchase. You may coordinate searching activities with a reference unit. You may work with a cataloging unit to be sure the catalog records contain enough detail for your unit to use to verify ownership of a particular item. In each of these venues, you want to represent the goals and needs of your team while sharing the concerns of other units with your group.

Pay attention to first meetings. As team leader, you will set the tone for how the group initially interacts. If you show that you are flexible, committed to team goals, and responsive to the group, you will set a positive tone that will carry the group through its first few meetings. By sending a clear signal that you support the team as a team, you will encourage the development of good team guidelines and processes.

Set clear rules for behavior. Help the group establish clear ground rules as they begin to coalesce as a group. Agreements on attendance, discussion options, confidentiality, meeting process, and other issues should be established early on in the process so team members can function effectively as a group while they build their skills to become a true team. Disagreements or resentments over simple items such as smartphone use during team meetings or the length of breaks can destroy team trust and make the group dysfunctional. A positive working environment that promotes true harmony within the team, without covering up tensions or disagreements, will lead to a productive team.

Spend lots of time together. As a leader, you need to spend time with your team. Absentee management will not work in a team environment. Delegating work to the group and then disappearing from the unit will not work. Team efforts require the group to work together. As team leader, you need to be a part of the group at the same time that you provide leadership and help set direction.

Provide positive feedback and constructive advice. As team leader, you are also responsible for providing feedback to the group. Team members need to know how they are performing as a group, how they are meeting goals,

FIGURE 7.2

Team Evaluation Tool

Rating Team Development

How do you feel about your team's progress? (*Circle rating*)

1. **Team's purpose**
   I'm uncertain — 1 2 3 4 5 — I'm clear

2. **Team membership**
   I'm out — 1 2 3 4 5 — I'm in

3. **Communications**
   Very guarded — 1 2 3 4 5 — Very open

4. **Team goals**
   Set from above — 1 2 3 4 5 — Emerged through team
   interaction

5. **Use of team members' skills**
   Poor use — 1 2 3 4 5 — Good use

6. **Support**
   Little help for individuals — 1 2 3 4 5 — High level of
   support for
   individuals

7. **Conflict**
   Difficult issues are avoided — 1 2 3 4 5 — Problems are
   discussed openly
   and directly

8. **Influence on decisions**
   By few members — 1 2 3 4 5— By all members

9. **Risk taking**
   Not encouraged — 1 2 3 4 5 — Encouraged and supported

10. **Working on relationships with others**
    Little effort — 1 2 3 4 5 — High level of effort

11. **Distribution of leadership**
    Limited — 1 2 3 4 5 — Shared

12. **Useful feedback**
    Very little — 1 2 3 4 5 — Considerable

SOURCE: Adapted with permission from Arnold Bateman, *Team Building: Developing a Productive Team* (Lincoln: University of Nebraska, 1990).

and how they are interacting. Effective leaders provide appropriate coaching, feedback, and advice even as they function as part of the team. (See the team evaluation tool in figure 7.2.)

Keep goals relevant. As team leader, you can help guide the group to ensure that agreed-upon goals and purpose mesh well with the overall goals of the organization. When teams are working on multiple goals, confusion can arise when goals appear to be in conflict. As team leader, you will need to watch for such situations and help coordinate or sort through team activities so that the team stays focused on the overall organizational objectives. Chris, as unit manager, knows that her organization values customer service. She also knows that there is a variety of ways to measure customer service. She works with her team, then, to develop goals for limiting the number of patron complaints or increasing the number of patrons served. Matching unit goals to organizational goals is crucial if the team is to remain relevant to the organization.

Create opportunities for others. Team leaders cannot take all the desirable assignments, praise, or glory and expect to have a successful team. Rather, true team leaders share opportunities, plum assignments, and rewards with the team. Watching staff develop into successful team members is a reward to a true team leader.

Do real work. Team leaders are important members of the team. While the role of team leader means that you have responsibilities outside of the team, you also have real work responsibilities inside the team. A team leader in interlibrary loan, for example, will help with lending requests or borrowing requests when needed and not just sit around while team members struggle to complete a day's set of requests.

Summary

Successful teams do not happen by accident. Building successful teams involves planning and effort. As a manager, before you embark on a team-building effort, assess your unit's readiness to be a team. Be sure the work of the unit fits well in a team environment. Evaluate the strengths of your staff and analyze the skills your unit will need to succeed as a team. Then, if the work and environment match the team concept, begin discussing the change to a team approach with your staff. Work together to develop strategies to become a successful team. By working together, your unit can move to a true team environment and will be successful in this different approach to managing the work of the group.

NOTES

1. Jon R. Katzenbach and Douglas K. Smith, *The Wisdom of Teams: Creating the High-Performance Organization* (Boston: Harvard Business Review Press, 2015), 41.

2. Edward Betof and Frederic Harwood, *Just Promoted! How to Survive and Thrive in Your First 12 Months as a Manager* (New York: McGraw-Hill, 1992), 128.

3. Glenn M. Parker, *Team Players and Teamwork: The New Competitive Business Strategy* (San Francisco: Jossey-Bass, 1990), 33.

4. Martin Broadwell and Carol Broadwell Dietrich, *The New Supervisor: How to Thrive in Your First Year as a Manager* (Cambridge, MA: Perseus Books, 1998), 273.

5. Katzenbach and Smith, *The Wisdom of Teams*, 89–91.

6. James H. Shonk, *Working in Teams: A Practical Manual for Improving Work Groups* (New York: AMACOM, 1982), 19–21.

7. Betof and Harwood, *Just Promoted!*, 131–32.

8. Adapted from Arnold Bateman, *Team Building: Developing a Productive Team* (Lincoln: University of Nebraska, 1990).

9. Elizabeth Fuseler Avery, Terry Dahlin, and Deborah Carver, *Staff Development: A Practical Guide*, 3rd ed. (Chicago: American Library Association, 2001), 125–46.

10. Betof and Harwood, *Just Promoted!*, 140–42.

11. Bob Pymm and Damon Hickey, *Learn Library Management*, 2nd ed. (Friendswood, TX: Total Recall, 2007), 107, 110, 111.

12. Linda Hill, *Becoming a Manager* (Boston: Harvard Business School Press, 2003), 297.

13. Broadwell and Dietrich, *The New Supervisor*, 268–69.

14. Bob Frisch, "When Teams Can't Decide," *Harvard Business Review* (November 2008), 121.

15. Ibid.

16. Ibid., 124–26.

17. Katzenbach and Smith, *The Wisdom of Teams*, 131–48; Broadwell and Dietrich, *The New Supervisor*, 270–71.

18. Scott Page, *The Difference: How the Power of Diversity Creates Better Groups, Firms, Schools, and Societies* (Princeton, NJ: Princeton University Press, 2008).

Planning and Organizing Work

Now that you are a manager, you are responsible for planning and organizing the work of your unit and those you supervise. Planning may include everything from day-to-day prioritizing of projects and activities for you and your staff to decision making on long-term projects and activities for your unit to meet your larger organization's goals. Planning is an ongoing process that must evolve as the needs of your organization change. You will need to be flexible and be a model of adaptability and flexibility for the staff you supervise, so that they become accustomed to the rapidly changing environment of today's libraries.

Setting Goals and Objectives

As the leader of your unit, you are responsible for ensuring that your unit has goals to accomplish. Goals should be practical activities that the unit can and should accomplish. These activities help order the efforts of the unit by providing a direction for the unit to follow. Without goals, the unit will not have direction and its members will not know if they are accomplishing tasks that will help the organization.

The goals of your unit or department should relate to the overall goals of your library or larger organization. Many libraries develop library-wide goals as part of a strategic planning process, an annual planning process, or some other planning effort. These goals may span several years, with new objectives developed for each year. Departmental goals can follow this pattern. As the manager of your unit, you will identify the goals of your unit or department, establish priorities among those goals, and identify the tasks that must be accomplished to meet the goals. It is important to include members of the unit in the goal-setting and objective-identification process. Staff in the unit provide firsthand knowledge and experience that can help shape the objectives for the unit and set measurable objectives.

Developing objectives for the unit becomes the basis for unit-wide as well as individual planning. Good objectives have the following characteristics, as summarized in the mnemonic SMART: specific, measurable, achievable, relevant, and time bound.[1]

An objective outlines specifically what is to be done (S) and what measures you will use to determine that an objective has been reached (M). The objective should provide the unit with a challenge that can be met (A). You don't want to write objectives that will serve to frustrate your unit because they cannot be completed. Objectives should support the mission, vision, and goals of the organization (R) and have a time frame attached to them (T). An objective for a reference department could be "to plan and implement a 24/7 online chat reference service within six months." The objective is specific (chat service, 24/7), measurable (either the service is implemented or it isn't), achievable (assuming the resources are available), relevant (it relates to user needs), and has a time frame (implement within six months).

Once you have identified goals and established priorities for your unit, you can determine your own personal goals and work with staff to determine their goals. You will need to decide who will perform each task, how often the task will need to be performed, and the timetables and deadlines for each task. Staff will need to understand the rewards for accomplishing the tasks and goals, as well as the implications for themselves and the department if tasks are not accomplished and goals are not met.

Remember to review and update your unit's action plans regularly, perhaps quarterly, to be sure you are on track for the year. By keeping your focus on overall objectives, you can be sure your unit does not get sidetracked by mundane details and day-to-day tasks and can accomplish the larger projects that bring success for your unit. With regular review of your unit's plans, you will be better prepared when the unexpected happens and unit goals need to shift. Being prepared and flexible will allow you to reprioritize when exciting new opportunities present themselves and to adjust as needed when less favorable changes are necessary.

Planning does not need to be an arduous process or one that induces sleep on the part of participants. As a supervisor, you can keep the process focused and efficient by following a few key steps.[2] These steps are the core of most planning processes. The first step is to list the external and internal forces that impact the unit. While many planning processes include a rather elaborate procedure for completing an environmental scan, you can do this with your unit rather easily as you think through the information you already know about your environment. Second, review the strategic initiatives of your organization. As a supervisor, you are not starting with a blank page when doing planning. You want to be sure your plans fit within the larger organization. Third, develop a list of activities for the unit that blend with the strategic initiatives of the organization. Finally, review the list of activities with the list of internal and external forces to develop a feasible set of objectives for your unit. You don't want to create objectives that cannot be completed, given the environment in which you operate.

How can this simpler process work for your unit? For Jamie, the metadata/cataloging unit head, this process will make it possible for him to create goals for his unit in two focused meetings. In the first meeting with his unit, Jamie and the group consider the external and internal forces that impact their work. External forces can include the economic outlook for the organization, changes from OCLC, implementation of a new library management system, new standards from professional associations, or the development and use of different metadata schemas. Internal forces can include budget reductions, possible restructuring proposals for the organization, and possible personnel changes as staff resign or approach retirement. The group also reviews the organization's strategic priorities, which could include decreasing expenditures, enhancing access to information resources, and ensuring a user-relevant catalog and discovery layer for access.

In the second meeting, Jamie and the group develop goals for the unit, such as incorporating metadata schemes for digital images into the workflow or reducing the use of paper by using more online communication among the unit's members. These objectives are specific and provide direction for the unit for the year. Finally, Jamie and the group review the goals along with the internal and external forces to ensure that the objectives are practical and achievable given the possible environmental changes. By staying focused on key activities, keeping conversations centered on achievable ideas, and not spending time on brainstorming ideas that cannot possibly be implemented, Jamie and his unit can create doable plans in a relatively short time.

Organizing the Work of Others

As a manager or supervisor, you will need to make decisions about how the work of your unit will be accomplished—what needs to be done and who will do it. As you will learn, most likely on your first day as a supervisor, each staff person is unique. Staff members will have varying backgrounds, experiences, and work styles, and supervisors must understand, recognize, and accommodate the different work styles of the people they supervise. The good news is that while individuals exhibit unique traits, there are some similarities in work style preferences. Some employees will prefer a great deal of structure; others will find too much structure to be stifling. Depending on your own style, you may need to adjust the way that you work with individual staff members. (See chapter 14 on motivation and chapter 15 on diversity for more about different work styles.)

Work style preferences can be generalized into two groups: creative types and structured types. As a supervisor, you will observe very different behaviors from these groups, and you may need to adjust your interactions with staff members of each type, depending on your own work style preference.

If you prefer a more structured environment, you may be frustrated when you supervise creative types even when the work is completed successfully. For example, creative staff members sometimes appear disorganized, yet often accomplish a great deal. The more structural aspects of work life, such as routines or work guidelines, may seem too mundane for creative types to follow. On the other hand, your creative staff members will bring new ideas to stale routines and, if you let them, help you to rethink the work of your unit.

To support creative staff members and help them to be productive, you might do the following:

> Present assignments in general terms, explaining the desired end result but allowing employees the latitude to find their own ways to that result. Establish timelines to keep productivity on track but don't structure the work process.

> Allow people to express risky ideas without immediately shooting them down. Saying, "Let me play devil's advocate" is the surest way to cut creative thinking off at the knees because it sets a negative tone. Instead, ask clarifying questions or begin with a phrase such as, "I am not in disagreement with the idea but want to explore some questions I have." This type of opening sends a more positive message and opens the door to discussion.

> Let people work through their mistakes to find their own solutions and allow time for this as part of the creative process. It takes a lot of coal to make diamonds.

> Learn how to praise someone's efforts without focusing on the result or product you want those efforts to generate.

> Ask employees what you can do to provide a stimulating and supportive environment. You might be surprised at how simple some of their requests will be.

> Sponsor workshops conducted by outside resources. Creative people are always looking to broaden the base of their knowledge and expertise. New faces bring fresh perspectives. Employees are sometimes more willing to question and raise issues with outsiders than they are with internal trainers or consultants.[3]

If you are a creative manager, supervising a staff person who wants or even requires structure can be frustrating. On the other hand, structural types are the people you want to help plan complex projects, as they are very skilled at breaking down projects into logical steps. They are good at implementation as well, and after understanding what the work is and what their roles are in the process, they will meet deadlines. Often their work spaces are neat and functional, and if necessary someone else can step into their jobs.

To help you determine how best to work with a person who needs structure, consider the following:

> Start by laying out specific tasks and the small goals that must be accomplished by the end of the day. Be sure the employee has the necessary tools to complete the tasks and knows how to use them.

> Identify common problems that might arise and establish a procedure for dealing with them. Some employees find it useful to have a chart or diagram that outlines the priorities and procedures, while others might just take notes.

> Meet with the employee at the end of the day to discuss how he or she approached the tasks and what actually got finished. Communication about expectations, and what worked and didn't work, is critical here.

> Establish procedures for identifying and addressing emergencies and unexpected changes in priorities. At first, this might mean having the employee come to you whenever work deviates from the planned schedule. As the employee becomes more skilled in structuring and adjusting priorities, the procedures might shift to general guidelines for when to contact you and when to proceed without assistance.

> Over time and as the employee's comfort with the structure progresses, designate daily tasks as part of the employee's routine, with the employee responsible for making them part of the workweek with less monitoring from the manager.

> Be a good model. Show employees how you prioritize your day, and then ask them to tell you how they would in turn prioritize their own. Then compare and show them how to make adjustments as needed.

> Follow up to see what works and what doesn't, first on a daily and then on a less frequent (but no less than weekly) basis.[4]

Planning a Day

In addition to planning the overall work of the unit, you also need to keep track of planning your own days and your own tasks to ensure you accomplish what you need to. David Allen suggests that each day there are three types of activities you might engage in:

- Doing predefined work
- Doing work as it shows up
- Defining your work[5]

Predefined Work

If you are taking action on items from your "to do" list or your next-action list, you are doing predefined work. That is, you are working on tasks that you previously determined need to be worked on. This might include preparation for a meeting with a staff member, drafting performance evaluations, and making or returning phone calls.

On-the-Spot Work

Some days it will seem as if you are not accomplishing anything from your list of tasks that need to be worked on because you have many interruptions. These interruptions, which Allen describes as doing work as it shows up, involve anything that comes up unexpectedly: a staff member stops by to talk with you about a workflow problem, or your boss needs some budget figures for an emergency meeting the next morning.[6] When you spend time on these interactions or tasks, you have prioritized these tasks, subconsciously or consciously, as more important than anything else you had planned to do at that time on that day.

Defining Your Work

Most library employees already spend time each day checking e-mail messages, reading paper mail, reading or writing meeting minutes, and responding to phone messages and voice mail. As a supervisor, you will add supervising staff and planning projects to this list. Some of these activities you will finish; many others will involve identifying action items or tasks that you will need to accomplish sometime. These daily tasks, most of which are routine happenings each and every day for supervisors, are what Allen calls defining your work; as you work your way through them, you will be adding items to your lists of tasks to accomplish.[7]

For example, it's late Friday afternoon and Chris, department manager, is reviewing her calendar and planning her work for the next week. She has three management meetings and a department meeting on her calendar. She also has individual meetings with five of her staff and she has two desk shifts.

She examines her schedule to identify blocks of time when she can work on projects. On her "to do" list she has three projects: prepare the unit equipment request, write two performance evaluations, and begin planning for a shift from print to electronic resources for the reference collection.

Next, she notes deadlines for the projects. The equipment request is due Tuesday, so she schedules a meeting with herself on Monday to ensure some uninterrupted time to work on the request. The evaluations are due in two weeks, so Chris knows she can work on these as time permits. Decisions on new electronic reference resources need to be made soon to meet the budget cycle deadline, so she wants to be sure that she has an outline of the process by the end of next week. This project includes coordinating activities with the acquisitions department, so Chris includes time for meetings with her counterpart in acquisitions to develop a timeline for the project.

By identifying a few key projects that need to be done and setting preliminary times to work on the projects, Chris has a good chance of getting the projects done. Without setting aside time for these projects, Chris could find her days taken up with daily tasks and interruptions that keep her from getting her own tasks done.

Meeting Deadlines

Deadlines are a fact of life. Without them, most people would not accomplish very much. As a manager, you will work with staff to determine the appropriate steps to meet deadlines.

For projects with a fixed deadline, one planning technique is backward planning. With backward planning, you start with the deadline and plan backward to the present time, developing a timetable listing the steps in the process. To do backward planning, you begin with the end event.

1. Make a list of tasks that must be accomplished before the deadline or event.
2. Working backward with a calendar, start with the last step.
3. Write the last step on the calendar and note any tasks that need to be accomplished by specific dates to make the last step possible.
4. Repeat #3 with the next-to-last step. Note related tasks.
5. Repeat #4 with next steps until you reach the first step.
6. Determine deadlines for each step.
7. Delegate related tasks to appropriate staff.

Backward planning, with deadlines for each step and delegation of steps to appropriate people, will help to ensure that no important steps or components of the process are overlooked. Also, backward planning will help all involved to know their roles and responsibilities and how much time it will take to complete the necessary tasks efficiently and effectively.

Projects for which backward planning might be appropriate include an event that must happen on a certain day and a project on which several staff members must participate for it to be successful. For example, you are the cataloging supervisor and you learn that an upgrade to the cataloging module of your online catalog system is scheduled for the end of the year. Once the date of the upgrade has been determined, you can plan backward from that date to make sure that everything is in place in time for the upgrade. Another example where backward planning could be effective is at the library service desk. Each semester, your unit prepares for the first day of the new semester, when records for new library users will be added to the online system. This year, everyone on campus will have a new ID card with a new identifying bar code. How much time do you have to make the necessary adjustments to routines? Whom do you need to involve in the discussions? What other campus units use the bar code and for what data? Answering these questions will help you as you develop your backward-planning outline.

Backward planning can also be used for smaller initiatives and for planning with staff members who work better when they have a structured workflow to follow.

Planning for Change

Many steps are necessary for successful change. For change to be truly successful, those involved must be able to see and understand why change is necessary. Change must be reinforced along the way. John Kotter and Holger Rathgeber propose an eight-step process for successful change:

- Create a sense of urgency.
- Pull together the guiding team.
- Develop the change vision and strategy.
- Communicate for understanding and buy-in.
- Empower others to act.
- Produce short-term wins.
- Don't let up.
- Create a new culture.[8]

Jamie walks into his regular biweekly meeting with the library director with his usual agenda items, expecting a typical meeting to review the budget and expenditures. Within seconds, though, he realizes something is amiss. Chris knocks on the director's door and pops her head in to ask if she's got the time wrong. Hasn't the director just called Chris to ask her to come by? Chris and Jamie look at each other, wondering what's up. Other managers begin to arrive. Their director is uncharacteristically rattled! Finally, she explains: she's just had a call from the budget office and learned that the library must immediately cut 20 percent from its operating budget; the library must make the cut in the next two months and plan for an ongoing cut of 10 percent for the next year's budget, which opens in four months.

Time is short! The director has created a sense of urgency—the library must have a plan in place within two months. During the next two hours, the director outlines the situation and she works with Jamie and Chris and the other managers (pulling together the guiding team) to decide how to handle the cuts (vision and strategy). They identify immediate cuts and develop a plan for determining the rest of the cuts, which will involve staff throughout the organization.

The director calls a staff meeting for the following day. All staff attend and she explains the situation: they must reduce costs and plan for a smaller budget for the next year. The director outlines the cuts that she and the managers have determined and asks all staff to work with their managers to find ways to meet the rest of the necessary cuts. The director and managers communicate with the staff for understanding and buy-in.

Jamie asks his metadata/cataloging staff to carefully review processing expenses and suggest short-term and long-term solutions to the funding shortfall. He asks that everyone take forty-eight hours to assess and then reconvene with their ideas. Chris meets immediately with her reference staff and asks them to focus on resources that duplicate other resources. Her group members agree to reconvene in one week with their ideas. Chris and Jamie empower their staff to act.

Both Jamie's and Chris's groups identify some quick fixes immediately, including drastically reducing binding and discontinuing print subscriptions for titles in large aggregator databases. All recognize these are not easy decisions, but they are decisions that must be made for the library to meet its budgetary obligations and thus successes in this change process. Chris and Jamie now must find ways to continue to lead the change effort, helping staff to find additional ways to trim expenses. Once the initial cost-saving measures are determined, Chris and Jamie will work with staff to continually review processes and procedures to be sure they create a new culture, one that makes new processes stick and helps everyone to be ready for future changes.

Time Management

Are you managing your time or is your time managing you? You may find that you ask yourself this question, as well as asking it of your staff. Much of what was discussed in the sections on setting objectives and meeting deadlines will help you to manage your time and the time of those who report to you. If reviewed regularly, calendars and action lists serve as effective time management tools for many people. Another technique, daily "to do" listing, is universal in traditional time management training. Key points for successful "to do" listing include the following:

- Each and every day make a daily list of "to do" items. Make it a habit.
- Add items from previous days that need follow-up.
- Prioritize tasks.
- Batch similar tasks.

- Keep "to do" readings on hand for when you have a few free moments.
- At the end of the day, use today's "to do" list to write tomorrow's "to do" list.[9]

Some management experts regard traditional "to do" lists as wastes of time. For example, David Allen prefers developing several lists, such as action lists, waiting-for lists, project lists, checklists, and someday/maybe lists.[10] Online calendar systems can also help you organize your time. You can use the "to do" function in the system to keep track of tasks that need to be done. Such systems can also keep track of deadlines and alert you to upcoming activities and meetings. For example, applications on mobile devices make it possible for you to keep your calendar with you so you can more easily manage your calendar and "to do" lists. You should determine for yourself the best system for you.

Project Management

Lee Cockerell, former executive vice president of operations at the Walt Disney World resort, and now a teacher for the Disney Institute, suggests a slightly different way to keep a "to do" list. He suggests people ask themselves the following questions when reviewing their "to do" lists: First, of everything I have to do in my life, which tasks should I work on today? Second, ask what projects do I start today that will pay off in five or ten years? Finally, what did I do yesterday that I may need to go back and do better?[11] These questions help supervisors think about long-term projects, work-life balance, and improving performance while establishing the list of tasks to do each day.

Other useful time management techniques include time analysis studies and group or team analysis. A time analysis study can be as simple as jotting down your activities during your workday. The format could be a chart with an hour-by-hour analysis of the way you spend each day for a certain time period. (See figure 8.1.) Another option is to use your personal calendar to note all activities worked on during times when you do not have meetings scheduled. This second option works best when your calendar system allows plenty of room for notes. Keeping a log of your activity for a set time period, one week or one month, for example, can be very revealing.

FIGURE 8.1

Sample Time Analysis Log

TIME	ACTIVITY	COMMENTS/NOTES

Careful analysis of your personal time log will allow you to see where you are spending your time and whether that time was well spent. Questions you might ask include these:

- Were you doing the right job at the right time?
- Could the job have been done at another time more effectively?
- Could you have delegated the job to someone else?
- What did you do that should not have been done at all?
- How much time did you spend online?

You may notice a pattern to the interruptions in your day. How are you interrupted the most often? Are the interruptions mostly by telephone? Are they from staff, colleagues, or your boss dropping in to see you? How often do you check your e-mail? Even e-mail, with you controlling when and how often you check it, can be an interruption.

Consider the frequency of these interruptions. How important were the interruptions? How long did it take you to get back to the task you were working on? You can control, to a great extent, the nature and type of interruptions. For example, set aside time each day to go through your inbox and respond to e-mail messages. For some people, checking their e-mail once in the morning and once in the afternoon is adequate. Others may need to do so more frequently. Regardless of your situation, when you check your e-mail, look for urgent messages and tasks that you can finish in less than two minutes. Urgent messages, of course, should be dealt with right away. Quick tasks can be finished and e-mails deleted. Other e-mail messages, which require reading or action that will take more time, can be deferred to the block of time you set aside each day for e-mail. This simple change will save you significant time and keep your e-mail inbox better organized.

Another important exercise to help you manage your time, and the time of your staff, is a group or team time analysis. The purpose of this exercise is to focus on what the members of your unit or group do that affects the use of one another's time. This exercise also requires a simple chart. To do the analysis, list all the people in your unit in the left-hand column. Note their

FIGURE 8.2
Sample Group Time Analysis

STAFF MEMBER	HIS OR HER ACTION	OTHERS' REACTIONS	PLAN TO REDUCE TIME WASTING
Bob	Visits with others on the way to and from break	Stop working to visit	Encourage Bob to schedule break times with people he wants to visit with
Gina	Extended telephone conversations	Overhear personal information and are uncomfortable	Remind Gina to limit personal calls
Rhonda	Asks numerous staff the same work procedure questions	Give different details, become frustrated with all the questions	Schedule a set time for Rhonda to visit with her supervisor to ask questions

actions. Note your actions. And in the right-hand column, note a plan to re-duce time wasting. (See figure 8.2.) A group or team analysis can be used to show how team members' actions both save and waste their colleagues' time.

Summary

The key to a less hectic work life is to organize, plan, and control your time. Annual plans begin with goals, objectives, and action plans with deadlines. Review progress regularly, at least quarterly. Monthly plans flow from the unit's action plans. Add regular activities, such as budget preparation dead-lines, to your list of tasks and projects to be sure you meet your responsi-bilities. Weekly and daily plans help you keep focused on what needs to be done. Tasks are less likely to fall between the cracks when you keep action lists and "to do" lists.

Check off or delete projects and tasks as you complete them. Celebrate the unit's completion of tasks and projects to help thank staff for their hard work and to reinforce the benefits of planning. Work closely with your staff to develop systems that help them be productive, stay focused, and complete tasks and projects in a timely manner.

NOTES

1. William A. Salmon, *The New Supervisor's Survival Manual* (New York: AMACOM, 1999), 78.
2. C. Patrick Kohrman II, "No Free Lunch: A Condensed Strategic Planning Process," *EDUCAUSE Quarterly* 31, no. 4 (2008): 62–65.
3. Gary McClain and Deborah S. Romaine, *The Everything Managing People Book* (Avon, MA: Adams Media, 2002), 93.
4. David Allen, *Getting Things Done: The Art of Stress-Free Productivity* (New York: Penguin, 2001), 97.
5. David Allen, *Getting Things Done: The Art of Stress-Free Productivity* (New York: Penguin, 2015), 21.
6. Allen, (2001), 8.
7. Allen, (2015), 44–45.
8. John Kotter and Holger Rathgeber, *Our Iceberg Is Melting: Changing and Succeeding under Any Conditions* (New York: St. Martin's, 2005), 130–31.
9. Mary Nofsinger, "Managing Work Time," in *Practical Help for New Supervisors*, ed. Joan Giesecke (Chicago: American Library Association, 1997), 83.
10. Allen, (2015), 50–51.
11. Lee Cockerell, *Creating Magic: 10 Common Sense Leadership Strategies from a Life at Disney* (New York: Doubleday, 2008), 161.

Budgeting Basics

Shortly after starting their new positions, Chris and Jamie meet for coffee. Chris has just received a budget report for her department and is confused about what she is supposed to do with the information she has been given. Because Jamie has been promoted from within the library, Chris hopes Jamie will know more about the budget system than she does. Chris shows the report to Jamie and asks him to explain it and suggest what she should do. Jamie looks at the report in confusion. The report Chris received does not look like the report he has for his unit. They realize that handling their units' budgets is going to take some background work to learn how to interpret the different reports they have and how these reports fit into the library as a whole. Now they have to figure out how to get the information they need. They decide to split responsibility for gathering information and then to meet again to compare notes.

The Big Picture

As a supervisor, you will have responsibility for parts of the overall library budget.[1] You may be responsible for a wide variety of budgets for your unit: a supply budget, a student wages budget, a salary budget, an equipment budget, or a professional development/training budget. Which aspects of the budget come under your responsibility will vary depending on your position and how your organization handles budgets. However, every supervisor needs to have a basic understanding of the overall institution budget in order to be sure that he or she is structuring the budgets she manages to reflect the larger organization.

It is imperative that unit or departmental budgets fit within the framework of the larger institutional or city/county budget. The overall rules for budgeting will come from the parent organization. These are used by the library administration to develop a budget for the library. Each supervisor will have responsibility for resources that he or she controls within his or her unit. To be effective as a supervisor, you need to understand the overall process used to create budgets before you can effectively design or monitor your unit budget.

Budget Methodologies

There is a variety of budget systems that may be used by the parent institution. Being familiar with these methodologies will be important as you develop your own budget.[2]

Planned program budgeting. A program budget lists all of the costs associated with each program and the results or outputs that the program produces. A program can be a service such as interlibrary loan. Interlibrary loan can be part of a larger unit or an independent unit, but in program budgeting, interlibrary loan services would be a budget category. The budget should include all the expenses associated with the program. For interlibrary loan, this might include such items as salaries, computer costs, OCLC costs, software costs, telephones, fax and scanner costs, supply costs, and even staff development costs. The outputs for interlibrary loan would be the number of items borrowed from other libraries, the number of items lent to other libraries, and the number of items sent to library users via an e-mail document delivery service. In assessing the program, you could determine the cost per output to determine what type of increase you may need to expand the program. In tough budget times, you could use the same data to determine the impact that a decrease in the budget has on the ability of the library to provide the service.

Incremental budgeting. Incremental budgeting is the process of requesting increases to a budget line based on last year's budget and on what is expected to happen in the next year. In a journals budget, for example, the budget request might be based on the amount of money spent on journals plus an average inflation factor. One can also divide the journals budget into different categories that might have different inflation rates and use these different rates to develop a more exact prediction on the cost of journals for the next year. For example, science, technology, and medical journals from European publishers may have higher price increases than humanities and social sciences journals. Conversely, some journals may have limits on inflation rates based on multiyear contracts. In doing the budget, you need to understand these differences and account for them in the budget request.

Zero-based budgeting. In zero-based budgeting, each program is evaluated as if it were a new program each year and had no historical budget. That is, the base budget is considered zero and the supervisor develops a new budget each year based on the program costs. Zero-based budgeting encourages an annual evaluation of each program in the library as supervisors consider every cost involved in a particular program.

A library may use more than one budgeting method to put together the overall budget request. The library materials budget may be treated as an incremental budget, with requests for increases based on predicted inflation factors. A new program may be submitted using a program-based budget to identify all of the costs associated with the new program. A zero-based budget may be used when a library needs to decrease costs and is trying to restructure the budget to cope with uncertain financial times. As a manager, it is important to work with the overall institution to know what type of budget request you need to put together and what information is needed for decision makers to decide how your unit will be funded.

Expenditures

It is also important to understand the different types of expenditures you may face. Some expenditures, such as utilities, are considered nondiscretionary costs that must be paid and over which most supervisors have little control. While you can effectively work with your unit to decrease utility costs by turning off lights, unplugging equipment during off times, or lowering office thermostats, as a unit manager you are not likely to have responsibility for ensuring that the utility bills are paid.

Some expenditures are more discretionary. These are the budgets that you as a supervisor will be able to influence and control. For example, a budget for student assistants or library pages is often the responsibility of a unit supervisor to monitor to ensure that the unit spends only the amount of money it has been allocated. A materials budget is another example of a discretionary budget, one the collections manager can control and, with subject librarians, use to determine the titles that will be purchased for the area. Again, the manager needs to be sure that expenditures do not exceed the budget allocation.

Often a supervisor is asked to put together a budget request for the next budget cycle. In putting the request together, the supervisor should review the overall goals and objectives for the library as well as the goals for his or her own unit to be sure that the budget request reflects the priorities of the library as a whole. For example, if the library has made a commitment to expand electronic reference resources, the department manager will want to put together a budget that emphasizes electronic resources rather than print resources. For a help desk service unit, the request for student assistants to help at the desk should reflect the hours of operation and the duties assigned to the unit. If student assistants sort and shelve materials as well as staffing a desk, the budget request should reflect how much time is needed for these two major duties so that the correct number of students can be hired to cover the unit responsibilities.

The budget request should provide a justification for the items in the budget as well as the dollars requested. Simply listing the dollar figure for student help will not provide the budget decision makers with adequate information to assess the request. The decision makers will want to know what tasks the students will cover, how many hours a week these tasks take, and how the budget will be expended throughout the year. Will more money be needed as school starts or will less money be needed around holidays or

FIGURE 9.1

Sample Budget Request

Rank	Preliminary Plans	Strategic Priority #1	Strategic Priority #2	Strategic Priority #3	Strategic Priority #4	Other	Total
	Library						
	FY18 Preliminary Budget Plan						
	Estimated Costs of New, Planned Strategic Actions						
	Submittal date:						
1	Restroom upgrade	1,100,000					1,100,000
2	HVAC					9,500,000	9,500,000
2	Main entry remodel—student-centered focus	100,000					100,000
	Salary and fringe benefit savings						-
2	Two new positions—data science librarians w/ benefits		150,000				150,000
3	New position—outreach librarian w/ benefits			75,000			75,000
3	New position—programming and events manager w/ benefits				65,000		65,000
							-
							-
							-
	Total Action Plans	**$ 1,200,000**	**$ 610,000**	**$75,000**	**$ 65,000**	**$ 9,500,000**	**$ 11,450,000**
	Key:						
	Rank: 1 = Must do (little choice); 2 = First priority; or 3 = Second priority						
	Strategic Priorities: 1 = Ensure access to the university experience; 2 = Enhance the university's research profile; 3 = Improve the quality of life for citizens; 4 = Continue to enhance and cultivate the university experience; 5 = Other						

school breaks? This type of question should be answered in the request so the decision makers do not have to guess at why you are requesting the budget you presented.

Also, be sure that your budget request reflects the reality of your unit. Ask yourself what changes have occurred in your unit that impact your budget. Has scanner use increased and printing and photocopying declined? What impact will an increase in the federal minimum wage have on the student assistant or page budget? Assessing each item in your request to be sure that it is still needed is an important though often overlooked part of preparing a budget. A sample budget request is shown in figure 9.1.

Budget Reports

While supervisors may not be responsible for using the institutional budget system, they still need to know the basic capabilities of the accounting and reporting system in order to know what questions can be answered from the system reports. For example, if you want to create a history of spending in your unit's equipment budget to show how you have been effective in addressing equipment needs, you will need historical data. Can the central system provide a report for your unit that breaks out your equipment requests? If not, do you have the data within your unit to put the report together? You need to know before you begin planning your budgets what information is available centrally and what information you will need to keep within your unit. On the other hand, you do not want to spend time creating shadow systems or unit-specific systems for reports or data that are available from the central system. It is not in your unit's best interest to spend time and resources recreating data that are easily available.

Monitoring Your Budget

Each library will have its own system for reporting on budgets. As a supervisor, you may receive a monthly report that tells you how much money you have spent in a particular category and how much money you have left. Some reports may help track encumbrances (items on order) as well as expenditures so you can be sure you do not overspend your budget because you forgot about ongoing or outstanding commitments. You will want to be sure that you understand how to read and interpret these standard budget reports and that you do so on a regular basis. A sample budget report is shown in figure 9.2.

If the library does not provide you with detailed reports to monitor your budgets, you will want to develop internal systems that help track your funds. A spreadsheet program can be used to develop relatively simple budgets as well as more complex budgets. You can create a relatively simple report for communications expenses for your unit. In the spreadsheet, you can record monthly use from the central reports and subtract the amount from the allocation. The spreadsheet can show the percentage spent. You can review the report for any unusual increases in monthly expenditures that are higher than anticipated. More complex reports can be developed to monitor multiple budget categories using linked spreadsheets. If you are not familiar with spreadsheet software, you may want to take a course to learn about the system or meet with someone in your library who knows the software in use at your organization. You may want to delegate responsibility for maintaining the budget spreadsheets to someone in your unit who is familiar with this type of software or responsible for a certain aspect of the budget. For example, the supervisor of student assistants might be a good choice for managing the student wage budget. But remember that as the unit manager you are responsible for the budget, so be sure you understand and review the

FIGURE 9.2

Sample Budget Report

Library Student Assistant Budget

CostCtr	$Allocation	$Wages_6-15-16	$Work.Study	SUM Wages/WS	Bal of $Alloc left 6-15-16	Est $ 6/16 thru 6/30/16	Est Bal of $Alloc left 6-30-16	Hrs_Alloc	Hrs_6-15-16	Bal of Alloc Hrs left 6-15-16	Est Hrs 6/16 thru 6/30/16	Est Bal of Alloc Hrs left 6-30-16
CIRC	$0.00	$48,444.63	($3,727.48)	44,717.15	(44,717.15)	0.00	(44,717.15)	6225.3	6225.3	0.0	0.0	0.0
DEANS OFFICE	$0.00	$928.50	$0.00	928.50	(928.50)	0.00	(928.50)	126.0	123.8	2.2	0.0	2.2
DESIGN	$0.00	$8,041.51	$0.00	8,041.51	(8,041.51)	340.00	(8,381.51)	1100.0	1070.9	29.1	42.5	(13.4)
DESIGN-SPECIALIST	$0.00	$6,575.23	$0.00	6,575.23	(6,575.23)	0.00	(6,575.23)	775.0	768.6	6.4	0.0	6.4
ELECT RESOURCES	$0.00	$10,479.44	($400.85)	10,078.59	(10,078.59)	274.40	(10,352.99)	1450.0	1398.6	51.4	34.3	17.1
STORAGE	$0.00	$8,355.57	$0.00	8,355.57	(8,355.57)	328.00	(8,683.57)	1000.0	959.0	41.0	41.0	0.0
MEDIA CENTER	$0.00	$20,611.84	($1,498.25)	19,113.59	(19,113.59)	0.00	(19,113.59)	2763.7	2763.7	0.0	0.0	0.0
PRES SERV	$0.00	$6,400.05	($552.75)	5,847.30	(5,847.30)	192.00	(6,039.30)	850.0	818.0	32.0	24.0	8.0
PROCTOR	$0.00	$31,188.73	($2,543.48)	28,645.25	(28,645.25)	0.00	(28,645.25)	3649.9	3649.9	0.0	0.0	0.0
SPEC COLL	$0.00	$17,677.22	($2,067.18)	15,610.04	(15,610.04)	1,224.00	(16,834.04)	2500.0	2323.8	176.2	153.0	23.2
STACKS	$0.00	$54,121.35	($3,151.25)	50,970.10	(50,970.10)	3,268.00	(54,238.10)	7664.0	7196.5	467.5	408.5	59.0
STUDENT SPECIALIST	$0.00	$5,161.60	$0.00	5,161.60	(5,161.60)	2,276.00	(7,437.60)	1859.8	581.1	1278.7	284.5	994.2
STUDENT SPECIALIST-WKLY	$0.00	$1,958.50	$0.00	1,958.50	(1,958.50)	996.00	(2,954.50)	300.0	248.0	52.0	124.5	(72.5)
TRAINING 24-7	$0.00	$144.70	($5.95)	138.75	(138.75)	0.00	(138.75)	0.0	16.8	(16.8)	0.0	(16.8)
VET MED	$0.00	$12,626.99	$0.00	12,626.99	(12,626.99)	496.00	(13,122.99)	1800.0	1644.9	155.1	62.0	93.1
VET MED-SPECIALIST	$0.00	$10,019.82	$0.00	10,019.82	(10,019.82)	48.00	(10,067.82)	1200.0	1140.8	59.2	6.0	53.2
Total 701 0901	$240,000.00	$242,735.68	($13,947.19)	228,788.49	11,211.51	9,442.40	1,769.11	33263.7	30929.7	2334.0	1180.3	1153.7

reports created by others. You are responsible for catching any problems and for ensuring that the reports are accurate and up-to-date.

Returning to Chris and Jamie

After a few weeks, Chris and Jamie meet again to go over the budget reports. Chris has learned that her unit is responsible for a reference materials budget, an equipment budget, and a student budget. She will be responsible for putting together a request each year for reference resources. She was advised that asking for an inflationary increase would not be an adequate request. Instead, she will need to put together a justification for the types of materials the unit needs, the subject areas to be developed, and the balance of print and electronic resources. Chris has decided that she will have a small committee in the unit help put the budget together, although this had always been done by the supervisor with the director. Chris wants to be sure that everyone in her unit understands how this important budget works.

Jamie has learned that each supervisor will need to track his or her own student budgets. Supplies are budgeted centrally, and Jamie will receive reports on supplies expenditures. Equipment budget requests will be submitted once a year. The request will indicate how the equipment will help the unit meet its goals and objectives. He has also learned that all public and staff computers are on a four-year rotation cycle, so individual supervisors do not need to budget for desktop computers for staff or for the public areas. Jamie explains to Chris that requests for specialized equipment are most successful if discussed first at leadership meetings and then included in annual department requests.

Further, Chris has learned that no one in her unit really understands budgets and spreadsheets. Jamie, on the other hand, has a number of staff who are experts in this area. They have agreed to share their expertise, and one of Jamie's staff will help one of Chris's staff set up a basic budget system for the unit. They also agreed to have a joint meeting with the library's accountant to review the budget systems they developed in their units in order to be sure they are creating and maintaining reports that will be compatible with the overall library budget and accounting system.

Summary

Monitoring the budget for your unit is a key task for today's manager. In these uncertain economic times, it is crucial for the supervisor to have accurate records and to anticipate change. If the institution might experience budget reductions, you will be better able to provide advice and help to senior management if you have a good grasp of your unit's budget and performance.

Work closely with your library's budget office to be sure you understand your budget and your budget reports. The budget is an area where it is much better to ask permission and to follow policies and procedures than to go off on your own and risk making budget decisions or purchases that are not permitted.

NOTES

1. For more information on budgeting, see Bob Pymm and Damon Hickey, *Learn Library Management*, 2nd ed. (Friendswood, TX: Total Recall, 2007), 113–20; and Pixey Ann Mosley, *Transitioning from Librarian to Middle Manager* (Westport, CT: Libraries Unlimited, 2004), 67–81.
2. Pymm and Hickey, *Learn Library Management*, 116.

Facilities, Space, and Safety

Debra J. Pearson

- Space Usage/Planning
- Safety: Surveillance, Disaster Planning, Evacuation, Shelter in Place
- Renovation/Construction
- Project Management
- Networking
- Summary

Libraries continue to evolve in terms of use and space allocation. As nonlibrary services and even retail outlets are finding themselves "embedded" in library space and less space is used to store print collections, the role of the facilities manager or planner has evolved from making sure lights are on and plumbing works to that of an integral part of the library's administrative team. As a manager, facilities management may be your whole responsibility or it may be combined with other duties, such as circulation, interlibrary loan, or stacks management. In any case, the ability to delegate and plan will be an asset in what can be a fairly stressful

DEBRA J. PEARSON is Associate Professor and Head of Libraries Facilities and Planning at the University of Nebraska–Lincoln.

environment. Most facilities management is learned on the job.[1] There are few opportunities for coursework in library degree programs. Sometimes it is alluded to in management courses, but in most cases, facilities management starts as "other duties as assigned," such as fielding calls from staff who have lights out in their offices, study rooms that are too hot or too cold, or a table with a broken leg. As more complex problems are presented, the person in a facilities management role becomes more familiar with whom to call and how to plan to avoid similar problems in the future, and in combination with learning library user and staff needs and desires for spaces in the building, the position becomes a permanent part of the person's list of responsibilities. Facilities management holds a unique place in the library's organizational chart. Liaison assignments can be moved to another subject specialist, library instruction is often the responsibility of librarians who chose that as their specialty, but facilities managers, as noted earlier, generally evolve into the job rather than applying for it.

Space Usage/Planning

Library users still expect the same things they always have from libraries: a place to study or do private research; a comfortable, safe place to wait between classes or appointments or to gather with friends; a place to find assistance with information gathering and analysis. Helping fill those needs are within the purview of the facilities manager.

It is in the best interest of the library to provide a variety of spaces. Do patrons want to work quietly and in isolation or in the middle of a busy, noisy environment? Do they want to work with friends or just have them nearby? Do they need to be able to plug in several devices with the expectation of an appropriate supply of outlets and a strong, reliable wireless signal? Do they want beverages and snacks? Do they have the expectation of being able to visit other academic, community, or retail services within the building? Are they hoping to find a space to meet friends for lunch and to plan social activities?

The level of success that patrons have with any of these needs is reliant upon a facilities manager having a role in space planning, being aware of what patrons need and want, and being able to provide the infrastructure so they have it. This requires knowledge of how patrons use space, being able to share that with the library administration, allocating the resources provided by the administration in a responsible way, and, last, providing ongoing maintenance of the building and equipment. It also involves building a network on campus that may include facilities, custodial services, building systems maintenance, landscape services, procurement (purchasing), police or security, fire and life safety officials, other types of code officers (e.g., Americans with Disabilities), as well as vendors and sales representatives.

Internal collaborators are important as well. If your library has a user experience staff member or committee, working with that person or committee can be a mutually beneficial relationship. Being in on the planning stages of events or new services can put the facilities manager ahead of the game in terms of preparing the space and making the event or service a success. Oftentimes, the facilities manager can inform staff about building issues that will need to be considered, such as a need for additional power or data, fire code issues (e.g., how many people can legally be in a room with only one exit), added duties for custodial services staff, or ADA compliance requirements for equipment or spaces, to name a few. Another internal partner is the staff member or unit manager in charge of shelving and/or print collections maintenance. Even though physical collections are being reduced in size, there is still a place for them in libraries, and they need to be kept in spaces that are appropriate for their long-term survival. Facilities managers and shelving/collections managers need to collaborate when working on space-planning projects to make sure that physical collections continue to be an integral part of the equation and not just an afterthought.

Perhaps the most important internal partner is the library director or dean. That person is the link between the library and the administration at an educational institution or the library board. It is imperative that you keep the dean or director apprised of projects you are working on, upcoming projects that will require funding, and ongoing maintenance costs, such as painting, repairs, replacement of furniture, additional custodial support, deferred maintenance or life safety items such as roofs or HVAC systems and elevators or fire alarm systems. In order to maintain appropriate resources to keep the infrastructure in optimum condition, the administration needs to be able to see why the money is being requested and how it is being spent in a responsible way. The director or dean is your advocate in that process.

Facilities management and space planning are also important when planning and maintaining office and service point spaces. As the use of the building has changed for patrons, so it has for the staff who occupy the rest of the space. For example, as fewer print volumes are purchased and more electronic resources become part of the virtual collection, not as much space is needed for book carts and shelves. What other purposes could that space fill? As work becomes more collaborative, fewer offices may be needed, thus freeing more area for spaces that require additional outlets, data ports, and furniture that can be reconfigured to accommodate different types and sizes of working groups. Facilities managers can help department managers, supervisors, and team leaders think about how to keep space flexible as job assignments for staff change.

Many service points are moving from a desk-centered model that provides only one type of service (e.g., circulation or reference) to combined service points that are comprised of freestanding tables and chairs that draw on the skills of user and reference service staff—a one-stop shop, if you will. Facilities managers serve an integral role in the planning of these spaces by providing guidance and advice on such things as floor boxes versus power poles, number of data ports, and furniture choices (adjustable? mobile? ergonomic?) and by helping staff navigate needs versus desires when it comes to design.

Besides library employees, other tenants of the building may include staff from other nonlibrary services, such as information technology or job/career placement services; retail tenants, such as a coffee shop or computer/bookstore; or outside staff who need to relocate for a few weeks or are occupying space for several months. In any case, many of the details involved in preparing the space for the tenants and helping them successfully integrate into the life of the building are the responsibility of the facilities manager. New staff will need to be oriented to the physical spaces of the building (where is the mail room? where is the break room?) as well as the operational aspects (what are the hours of the building? how do they get in and out after hours? how do they report problems? what is the mailing address of the building?). Facilities managers can serve as the "welcome wagon" for new staff.

Safety: Surveillance, Disaster Planning, Evacuation, Shelter in Place

Personal, collection, and building safety is not a guarantee. A library is not always a safe space for patrons or the staff who work there. As has been demonstrated time and time again, a public building offers free access to people who have their own agendas. Sometimes their agendas are not in the best interest of the public. This is especially true for libraries. They are considered places for community users or students to come for valid reasons as well as some of a more questionable nature. It often falls to the facilities manager to provide a sense of safety for building occupants. Because one person cannot be expected to know what is going on in an entire building all the time, the front line is staff. As facilities manager, you should plan to enlist their cooperation in keeping their eyes and ears open and alerting the proper authorities when they observe someone or something that makes them suspicious. Using situational awareness—the ability to take in information about those around you and your surroundings—as well as self-analysis to interpret that information and act accordingly is an important skill to develop and elicit in members of your staff.[2]

In addition to this internal surveillance tool, mechanical surveillance in the form of strategically placed cameras is also an option that should be explored. Facilities managers should work with trained personnel (vendors or police trained in surveillance) to ascertain what type of camera to use, how many to install, and where to place them throughout the building(s). Budget is often an issue, so it is even more important to be sure that you are getting the broadest coverage possible with the fewest number of devices. Special attention should be paid to entrances, exits, secluded areas, areas where valuable collections or artifacts may be displayed, or areas that have already been identified as prone to thefts, improper activity, and so forth.

Having a positive relationship with local law enforcement is invaluable. While some libraries may find it necessary to have a law enforcement officer as part of the staff, others may not be able to do so due to budgetary or personnel restrictions. In those cases, working with local law enforcement to apprise them of what issues may arise and to establish a routine walk-through schedule (but not so rigidly scheduled that people know when to expect them) may be sufficient for your building(s).

Disaster planning can be the sole responsibility of the facilities manager, or he or she may serve on a broad-based disaster team, depending on the size of your staff and the type and size of your collection. Disaster planning is a complex and important topic.[3] Like facilities management, disaster planning is not something that is generally taught in library school, although aspects of it may be part of a preservation or conservation program. Taking the time and making the effort to become aware of the issues, best practices, policies, and procedures involved in disaster preparedness is in your and your library's best interests. In this case, learning on the job is not the best way to go.

Creating a disaster plan is a must, and that plan should not be created in a vacuum. Using a template can help you cover all the bases, and the plan should be tailored to your collection and the needs of your users. One general question to ask is this: Does your collection contain more physical or digital pieces? Preservation and restoration of digital files may be more important than saving/restoring physical pieces. Value to the overall collection versus time and money to preserve or restore items is a point to be considered. This is especially important when discussing microformats. Many of those resources may now be available digitally. Other questions to consider include these: How many unique pieces does your collection have? Do you have archives? How many items in your general collection are unique? How should those be identified prior to a disaster and dealt with in the face of one? How will staff and users safely evacuate the building? How will the safety of staff and other responders be addressed during the reclamation/recovery period?

Be aware, going in, that no disaster plan covers every possible scenario of what can go wrong. However, having even a basic plan is better than having no plan at all. The disaster plan should be reviewed and updated every two to three years—sooner if library spaces, buildings, or services undergo major changes (e.g., the construction of a storage facility or the elimination of library collection space to make way for more user space). Another cause for review is if members of the disaster team change through retirement, resignation, or reassignment.

Evacuation and shelter-in-place procedures are often part of disaster planning and building safety. Here is another instance when all occupants of the library need to be aware of proper procedures—what the evacuation/shelter-in-place plan is, what warrants the plan being activated, how to put the plan into action, and what to do during and after the situation. Working with a trained professional will save you time and produce a more effective plan than trying to figure out things on your own. Most police departments or city offices have experts who are happy to visit your building(s), walk through with you, and identify appropriate evacuation routes as well as help you develop a shelter-in-place plan and provide training and/or training materials. They can assist in identifying doors that should be "exit only," rooms that can be locked from the inside for sheltering in place, and a gathering place for staff if leaving the building is the best option, for example. Conveying this information to all staff, and especially to those staff who work directly with patrons, is crucial. Drills of procedures for both evacuation and sheltering in place should be held on a regular basis. Working with the library administration to enlist support for full participation of staff is vital.

Renovation/Construction

At some point, you may be fortunate enough to be involved in renovation of existing space or construction of a new space. While the prospect of such large projects can be daunting, the reality is that it provides a great opportunity to guide the look and function of one of the main services on a campus or in a community for years to come. It also provides you with an opportunity to learn from the architects, construction workers, landscapers, and other trained and skilled staff who will work with you for the duration of the project. Do not waste that opportunity! As with disaster planning, the broad discussion that is needed to cover the topic is outside the scope of this chapter. However, a few comments here may provide some help should you find yourself on a planning committee and then as one of the point people working as a library advocate during the construction.

The library administration is the owner of the building, not the construction company. You will need to work with the dean or director and the senior administrative team to establish what will be acceptable when the construction crew is in your building. These parameters should be clearly delineated at a kick-off meeting. Perhaps the most common challenge is that construction workers do not always realize what working in an occupied building means. Other items that can cause some friction are where the staging area will be, particularly if the workers are expecting to use space in your building, and where construction workers can and cannot park (they seem to gravitate toward loading areas and docks). You will need to make clear and document what behavior is expected, which oftentimes will need to be repeated throughout the process. Obviously, the building will not be as clean or as quiet as you would prefer, but neither should you have to deal with continually asking that radios be turned down or off or picking up fast food trash, and so on. Go for a happy medium. Obviously, safety concerns, such as tripping hazards, electrical or plumbing violations, and so forth, should be addressed immediately.

Work through channels. Introduce yourself to the project manager, the construction manager(s), and the crew chiefs for subcontractors. Make sure you let them know that if they have questions about anything that would affect the library (e.g., working after hours, power or water outages, fire systems down for inspection, access), you are the initial contact, and conversely, if you have questions about any aspect of the project, ask to whom those concerns should be addressed for the most timely response.

Do not expect that everything will be done to your satisfaction when the construction workers are called to the next job. Keep a "punch list," a list of unfinished items, and make your project manager, building inspector, and the construction company's project manager aware of those items that still need to be finished. If there is a "warranty" period after the completion of the project, ascertain which items can be addressed by local facilities personnel and which need to be reported to the construction manager as a warranty issue. Document items that have to be called in repeatedly and report those to the project manager for quicker resolution. Any costs for repairs that are not made during the warranty period will come out of the library budget, so it is imperative that those items are addressed in a timely manner.

Welcome the assistance of professionals. If selecting furniture, finishes, wall/floor coverings, and so on, is part of your charge as facilities manager, solicit the advice of interior designers, sales representatives, and the purchasing agent the university or city assigns to you. Their expertise is invaluable, and coupled with your knowledge of how users inhabit the building, the selections you are responsible for have a greater chance of providing both comfortable, appropriate spaces for users and décor that will pass the test of time, both in terms of style and durability.

If possible, visit showrooms to see the items. Ideally, vendors will provide samples of smaller pieces to try out to see if they are really appropriate for the space you have in mind. There may be similar pieces in other buildings on your campus or in your community. Drop by to take a look and talk to staff members in other areas to see what their impressions are of the use and durability of the pieces. You may think twice based on these remarks—or not.

Keep custodial staff in the loop. The custodial staff will be responsible for daily maintenance of the building. Let them know early on that there will be additional space or existing space that will be used differently, so they can integrate those changes into their budget, personnel, and equipment scheduling. This is especially important if you are moving to a 24/7 or other nontraditional schedule and the custodial department has staff available only Monday through Friday. If possible, include them in the space planning and equipment selection (such as bathroom accessories) portion of the process, and make sure they are invited to tour the facility early and often. Make sure, as best you can, that the construction company is made aware of specific types of equipment that the custodial department uses if the products will be supplied as part of the project. An example is paper towel dispensers. The custodial department may use a certain size and type of paper towel roll and a type of dispenser the project supplier does not carry. Many modifications may need to be made before the dispenser will operate reliably with the specific roll. In hindsight, it would have been easier if the custodial department had supplied the dispenser or the architect/construction company would have asked the custodial department what size paper would be used. Making sure that the materials selected can be easily cleaned and that adequate numbers of garbage and recycling receptacles, paper towel dispensers, and storage for custodial equipment and supplies is paramount to keeping the space looking and operating at its best. Establish a positive rapport with custodial staff and supervisors so that problems can be addressed and resolved quickly or at least identified for further review.

Have a plan but stay flexible. Construction projects often involve timelines, contractors, and many other moving pieces, so delays outside your control may happen. Stay in communication with all parties and be prepared for changes. Do not plan a grand opening based on the completion date you hear before the project begins.

Celebrate! When the project is complete, welcome your community in to show them what has been accomplished. All the noise, dust, odd smells, extra people, and mess will have been worth it.

Project Management

A facilities manager has the potential of having several projects going on at once. Some may involve general upkeep, such as painting or replacing plumbing fixtures. Others may involve moving staff into new offices or work spaces or space planning for merging departments or service points. Throw in planning a new building or renovating existing space, and it becomes apparent that some sort of organization beyond "to do" lists is necessary. This is where project management comes in. Project management is a methodical approach to planning and guiding project processes from start to finish.[4] According to the Project Management Institute, the processes are guided through five stages: initiation, planning, executing, controlling, and closing.[5]

As with disaster planning, dozens of books and websites are devoted to this topic, so a simple summary is presented here.[6] Briefly, the process includes establishing a team, writing a proposal, identifying stakeholders and timelines, and concluding with an evaluation when the project has been completed. It sounds convoluted and cumbersome at the outset, but the process is invaluable when establishing lines of communication, delegating tasks, and making sure that all interested parties are aware of and have had input into the process. The evaluation portion assures that the project accomplished what was identified in the proposal, and that it met the budget and deadline established at the outset or that adjustments were made along the way.

A well-done project management plan keeps all stakeholders in the loop, prevents "scope creep," and documents action items, timelines, budgets, and change orders as the project moves to completion. It allows a facilities manager to provide information to stakeholders or project partners on short notice and makes sure that details are not overlooked due to information overload and lack of organization.

Networking

As mentioned at the beginning of the chapter, facilities managers are usually made, not hired. Creating local networks of internal and external partners is vital to the successful manager. Much of the learning takes place on the job. Conferring with others in similar positions can sometimes keep one from "re-creating the wheel." Happily, such colleagues are becoming easier to find. In the past few years, facilities management has begun to appear as a topic for meetings and conferences, often bundled with discussions on space planning. The American Library Association (ALA) includes some facilities planning meetings as part of the Building and Equipment Section of LLAMA (Library Leadership & Management Association).[7] The ALA and LLAMA websites have quite an array of useful information. State or regional annual library conferences often include programs on facilities and space planning. Many private companies offer multiday sessions that include visits to newly renovated or constructed libraries along with short courses on project management, assessment of space, and other facilities-related topics. While these may be expensive, they do provide a lot of information in a short span of time and put you in a networking situation that is hard to beat. Simply calling the director of a library you have heard has undergone some changes and asking to come by for a visit is generally welcomed. We love to show off our spaces!

Summary

Facilities management has become an increasingly visible and important part of the library organizational chart. Whether facilities management is considered "other duties as assigned" or identified as a full-time or part-time component of a position, it is generally a unique position in an organization. To do it well requires a working knowledge of and interest in how libraries operate in the "organizing information" sense. In addition, a facilities manager needs to have that same working knowledge of and interest in the operation and structure of the buildings itself. Both elements are important to the process of providing patrons with a safe and comfortable place to take the best advantage of the resources—physical, digital, and human—that are found there, and to providing both patrons and staff with the assurance that someone is available and able to address their concerns for comfort and safety.

NOTES

1. For more information on facilities management, see Donald A. Barclay and Eric D. Scott, *The Library Renovation, Maintenance, and Construction Handbook* (New York: Neal-Schuman, 2011); and Carmine J. Trotta and Marcia Trotta, *The Librarian's Facility Management Handbook* (New York: Neal-Schuman, 2001).
2. Chris Ray, "Situational Awareness" (blog post), PreparedChristian.net, March 13, 2012, http://preparedchristian.net/situational-awareness/#.WH5_mH06GSp.
3. For more information on disaster planning, see Camila A. Alire, *Library Disaster Planning and Recovery Handbook* (New York: Neal-Schuman, 2000); Miriam B. Kahn, *Disaster Response and Planning for Libraries*, 3rd ed. (Chicago: American Library Association, 2012); and Johanna Wellheiser, Jude Scott, and John Barton, *An Ounce of Prevention: Integrated Disaster Planning for Archives, Libraries, and Record Centres*, 2nd ed. (Lanham, MD: Scarecrow Press and Canadian Archivists Foundation, 2002).
4. WhatIs.com, "Project Management" (definition), SearchCIO.TechTarget.com, accessed January 17, 2017, http://searchcio.techtarget.com/definition/project-management.
5. Project Management Institute, "What Is Project Management?," PMI.org, accessed January 17, 2017, www.pmi.org/about/learn-about-pmi/what-is-project-management.
6. For more information on project management, see Joseph Heagney, *Fundamentals of Project Management*, 5th ed. (New York: AMACOM, 2016); Cynthia Stackpole Snyder, *A Project Manager's Book of Forms: A Companion to the PMBOK Guide*, 5th ed. (New

York: Wiley, 2013); and Cynthia Stackpole Snyder, *A User's Manual to the PMBOK Guide*, 5th ed. (New York: Wiley, 2013).

7. American Library Association, "LLAMA Buildings and Equipment Section," ALA.org, accessed January 17, 2017, www.ala.org/llama/sections/bes.

Managing Meetings

As a library employee, you attend many meetings. As a manager, there may be days when you question whether you ever do anything but attend meetings. It has been estimated that many supervisors spend at least one-third to one-half of their work time in meetings.[1] Often, as a manager, you will chair or lead meetings. While chairing meetings may sometimes seem like a daunting task, the skills for effective meeting management can be learned.

You will participate in many different types of meetings. Some of your meetings will be regularly scheduled sessions with individual staff members. You may also lead your department or unit meetings. Some meetings will be called to address specific topics. Others may be open-ended sessions, with the intent to brainstorm ideas about future directions. Other meetings may be regularly scheduled for the same time each week. You may also find that you are having more virtual meetings, during which you and other participants are not in the same location but are connecting by conference call or Web technology. The skills necessary for effective meeting management can apply to many, if not all, types of meetings, and once you have learned them, you will be ready to lead productive meetings.

The Basics of Meetings

The following key points apply to any meeting:

> *Purpose.* Meetings should have a purpose. First, be sure you have a reason to meet. Do not waste people's time by holding a meeting that has no purpose.

> *Timing.* Begin meetings on time. We all have busy schedules. Starting and ending meetings on time will signal that you respect participants and value the time of the people at the meetings.

> *Organized.* Most meetings should last no more than one hour. But if they need to run longer, try to keep them to no more than two hours. Meetings that go on longer than an hour or two may become repetitive instead of constructive.

> *Agenda.* Develop and share agendas prior to meetings. Agendas alert participants to the topics to be covered and give participants time to prepare for meaningful discussion.

Meetings with Individual Staff

For supervisors who are new to an organization or new to a supervisory role, initial orientation meetings with all unit members are particularly important because they help to set the tone for the supervisors' work with the unit. As a supervisor, you can use a set list of questions to ask each member of the unit as your agenda for the meetings. While it is not necessary to rigidly follow the list of questions, you should try to cover as many of them as possible. First of all, you need the information the answers will give you, and secondly, staff members will likely compare notes about the meetings. At these initial orientation meetings, it is important to keep the discussion focused on work-related topics. By asking everyone the same questions, you will be seen as a fair and impartial supervisor, interested in the opinions and viewpoints of all.

Because Chris is new both to her supervisory position and to the organization, the questions she might ask during the orientation meetings may vary slightly from those asked by Jamie, who worked in his unit prior to being promoted to his new position as supervisor. Questions Chris may want to ask of each staff person include the following:

> What are your areas of responsibility?
>
> What are your top priorities?
>
> Do you have problems or concerns that I should know about?
>
> What are your expectations?
>
> How satisfied are you with the way the department is currently running?
>
> What is the workload? Is it reasonable?
>
> Are there areas of interest that you would like to pursue?
>
> How satisfied are you with your current position?
>
> Is the position description up-to-date?
>
> Do you supervise others? How is that going?
>
> Do people have the right equipment and skills to do their jobs?
>
> What resources are you responsible for?
>
> What other departments does your work impact?
>
> Do you have concerns about other departments or units that I should be aware of?
>
> What is your view of the organization's goals and objectives?
>
> What is your career plan?
>
> What changes would you recommend be considered?
>
> What else do I need to know about you, the department, or the organization?[2]

Because Jamie has worked in his unit previously, he may already know the answers to some of these questions. For example, he likely knows each staff member's responsibilities, the resources available to them, whether they also work in other units or departments, and so on. Jamie should take care, however, not to assume that he already knows everything about each of the staff who now report to him.

Depending on your own situation, and how you came to be a manager in your current organization, asking these questions of your staff members will help inform you as you develop an understanding of your unit.

After the initial orientation meetings with staff, you will want to plan for regular meetings with staff members who report directly to you. These meetings will help you to stay up-to-date with the work of your unit, allow you to develop good working relationships with staff, and provide early indications of both successes and failures. As you learn more about your staff members, you will be in a better position to assess their skills, knowledge, and competencies at performance evaluation time, as well as their unique talents that may be instrumental in moving the work of your unit forward.

Individual staff meetings should take place as frequently as necessary to provide you with enough information to know whether a staff member is accomplishing his or her work. Depending on your proximity to staff work spaces, you may be able to informally assess staff progress and decide that meeting formally can happen less frequently. In some situations, though, it may be necessary to meet weekly or biweekly. Some organizations have guidelines around how often to schedule regular meetings with direct reports. Furthermore, as addressed in the chapter 4's discussion of performance appraisal, addressing and handling performance problems will take additional meetings.

Unit or Department Meetings

Once you have oriented yourself to the unit and learned more about its culture and traditions, it will be much easier to lead unit meetings. While scheduling regular meetings for your unit is important, the necessary frequency of these meetings will vary for several reasons, including the size of your unit, your unit's place in the larger organizational structure, and simply the mechanics of arranging a meeting and the logistics of staff schedules.

If the unit is small, with fewer than five individuals, frequent formal meetings may be unnecessary, particularly if your work areas are situated near one another and the unit has a culture of close communication and collaboration. Unit members may be in close contact with you and with one another and will need communication solely about events and issues of the larger organization.

However, whether large or small in staff size, any unit that is part of a large organization will need regular communication about the larger organization, and meetings are an effective way to share this information. E-mail and staff intranet sites have made it much easier to share news, particularly for large organizations. However, as a supervisor, you are responsible for communicating news to staff, and regularly scheduled meetings will help you increase communication. Unit meetings provide an opportunity for two-way communication—overall organization to unit and vice versa.

For some units, the nature of the work completed by the unit may help determine the frequency of the meetings. In an environment of quickly changing priorities, frequent meetings are crucial. For a unit embarking on a new project or program, regularly scheduled meetings are necessary for planning purposes and to stay on target. Finding a regular meeting time can be a challenge for all supervisors, whether they supervise public-facing service operations or behind-the-scenes technical services or systems staff. Supervisors of public-facing operations, where desks are open and staffed all hours that the library is open, may find it very difficult to schedule a meeting time that works for all staff members. In these situations, a supervisor may need to rely on student workers or assistants to staff desks. Another alternative is for a supervisor to lead the same meeting twice. While this does allow for 100 percent participation, it may lead to miscommunication. Other staff, in units such as technical services or automated systems, may have flexible schedules and alternate work sites. Although it may be difficult to plan a unit meeting at least once a month, your job of supervisor will be easier if you can accomplish having meetings on a regular basis.

Preparation for Meetings

Effective preparation is the key for all meetings. As a supervisor, you will often be in a position to determine or define the purpose of the meeting and to remind all participants to follow meeting guidelines. For an example of meeting guidelines, see figure 11.1.

FIGURE 11.1
Library Meeting Ground Rules

1. Distribute agenda in advance.
2. Set agenda action goals and discussion time limits.
3. Start on time; end on time.
4. Come to the meeting prepared.
5. One person speaks at a time.
6. Expect/respect differences.
7. Everyone participates; no one dominates.
8. No side conversations; stay on task.
9. Disagree in a respectful manner.
10. Disseminate/archive minutes in a timely manner.

Used with permission of the Iowa State University Library.

Meetings for Information Dissemination

For some meetings, the purpose may be simply to communicate news and directives from the larger organization. These meetings are sometimes called information and briefing meetings.[3] For example, you may schedule meetings with your unit to relay information from a larger departmental or organizational meeting you have attended. The purpose of the meeting is to communicate organizational issues to your unit. Distributing an agenda prior to the meeting, with basic details about the content of the meeting, will convey your purpose to the participants.

Planning, Problem Solving, and Other Issue-Driven Meetings

You may schedule meetings for purposes other than communication with unit members. These meetings can be planning workshops for an upcoming project or initiative, problem-solving sessions for new workflow routines, or even decision-making meetings for issues that require group discussion.

For special topic-driven meetings, you will be most successful if you state objectives and expectations for the meeting ahead of time. As with the

FIGURE 11.2
Sample Meeting Agenda

The Technical Services Committee will meet on Tuesday, March 16, at 9:00 a.m. in the library conference room.

Agenda

Approval of minutes from the 3/1 TS Committee meeting

Strategic planning—update from library-wide Planning Committee (20 minutes)

Review of revised flextime policy (10 minutes)

Holiday hours (5 minutes)

Student assistant budgets—reminder of year-end spending (2 minutes)

Quarterly projects (15 minutes)

Other (3 minutes)

Announcements (5 minutes)

---

regular information briefing or communication meetings mentioned earlier, topic-driven meetings should include an agenda that is distributed to all participants prior to the meeting. The agenda can be quite simple or very detailed, depending on the topic and type of meeting, although it will most often be more detailed than the agenda for a regularly scheduled unit meeting. Figure 11.2 shows a sample agenda for a meeting.

Other important steps to plan for include choosing an appropriate time and location for the meeting and arranging the meeting room in an appropriate manner to allow all to participate. For many small-group meetings, a circle or square will be most conducive to active participation. For large-group meetings, it may be necessary to use a different seating arrangement, depending on the size of the group.

The last step in meeting preparation is to be certain that all meeting participants, the staff you supervise, know where and when the meeting will take place. Having regularly scheduled meetings in regular locations takes away the guesswork for staff, and they and you can plan their work and manage their time accordingly.

Conducting the Meeting

At the beginning of the meeting, greet staff and help them to feel welcome. Make sure staff members with special needs have appropriate accommodations. For example, a hearing-impaired staff person may need to sit directly in front of you if he or she reads lips, and a staff person with mobility concerns may need greater aisle width. These issues should be considered prior to the meeting, when you are determining the meeting room and furniture layout.

Start on time. Through careful attention to the agenda, you will be able to accomplish much during your meeting. Encourage discussion and feedback and keep the conversation on topic. Take notes during the meeting. For meetings with formal minutes, consider assigning this responsibility to a staff member or seek volunteers from among the participants. Minutes should be shared with all participants prior to the next meeting. At the conclusion of the meeting, summarize key points, repeat action items and individuals' responsibilities, and set the date, time, and place for the next meeting. Finally, end on time.

Skills for Handling Problem Behaviors during Meetings

Sometimes meetings just do not go well despite your best intentions and attention to all of the premeeting details. The reasons for this might include participants who do not want to participate, someone with a hidden agenda, the wrong people "at the table," and perhaps a lack of leadership manifesting itself in a meeting that seems out of control. There are several communication strategies that you, as meeting leader, can use to help meetings flow smoothly and be successful. These techniques include active listening, clarification, summarizing, acknowledging the intensity of feelings or emotions, reframing, and the use of "I" statements.

Active Listening

To listen actively, you convey interest in what you are hearing, restate the speaker's ideas, reflect the speaker's feelings, and then summarize what you are hearing: "So, you are saying that the new organizational structure is troubling you. I can see why you might feel worried about your place in the new department. Let's talk more about . . ."

Clarification

You can use open-ended questions to clarify what you are hearing. This will help you to learn more about the situation and to begin to identify issues. An open-ended question might begin with, "Tell me more about . . ." With clarification, it is important to focus on the issues, not you or the person who is speaking. Be careful not to imply judgment in your questions. Try to find something of value in everything that is said.

Summarizing

Summarizing allows you to pull together all of the facts before moving on in your discussion. This helps to clarify what has been said and agreed to. It also allows the group to reach consensus and move forward or to recognize that more discussion is needed. "Before we move on, let me review what I think we've decided so far. We agreed to start the new process on February 1. Joe and Jim will work together to update our policy documents. Jerry will work with the systems office to load the new software on our computers. I will alert the other departments that February 1 is the start date. We agreed to meet once each week until February. And, finally, we will assess how the new process is working on February 15. Does that cover all the details we discussed?"

Dealing with Emotions

It is important to recognize that sometimes feelings and emotions are an integral part of the message being conveyed. Acknowledging the intensity of the feelings or emotions can be helpful in understanding and resolving the issue. Reframing, along with acknowledging and paraphrasing, are two communication techniques that can help with emotional messages. Reframing neutralizes the messages, making them more acceptable to the listeners. Reframing can be used to increase or decrease the emotional level and, if necessary, to remove the emotion from the content. Consider these examples:

> If you hear, "There is no way we can possibly pull this off by the end of the month," you might reframe this by saying, "So, you think this won't work. Why not?"

> If you hear, "He never listens to me," you might reframe this as, "It sounds like you're frustrated with Joe."

These reframed comments will encourage the speaker to reply, possibly providing you with more information or insight into the problem. Reframing separates the person from the problem.

Acknowledging and paraphrasing is another active listening technique that allows you to let the staff person know that you heard what he or she said, that you understand the intensity of his or her feelings, and that having those feelings is okay. This technique can be difficult to master. Stating that you understand the staff member, or his or her problem, is not necessarily acknowledging it. There are situations in which you will not want to recognize the emotional aspect of the message. For example, your department is discussing a new work schedule that requires that more staff arrive at 7:00 A.M. to work on a computer upgrade. Mary, an older employee, is frustrated with Joe, a younger employee, who is always late for these early morning projects. "You cannot trust him to show up," she says. Now is not the time to acknowledge Mary's emotion. Instead, try summarizing the issue by asking the group how they can be sure everyone arrives on time to help. In these situations, it will be more effective if you use another communication technique, such as reframing or summarizing, rather than acknowledging and paraphrasing.

"I" Statements

"I" statements are used to describe your feelings, to describe behavior in neutral and descriptive terms, and to describe the results of the behavior. In positive situations, for example, when you are telling a staff member how much you appreciate his or her work, "I" statements can be very powerful motivating messages. For example:

> "I am so pleased . . . when you jump in to help plan new projects . . . because I value your opinion and experience."

> "I am so glad . . . you came to the meeting and participated . . . because I know how important this issue is to you."

In negative situations, "I" statements are useful because you can convey how strongly you feel about the situation. For example:

> "I feel frustrated . . . when you forget to close out the cash register . . . because I know you are aware of the library's policy."

> "I am frustrated . . . when you don't participate at meetings . . . because I know you have valuable input to share."

After the Meeting

Minutes

As soon as possible after the meeting, distribute meeting notes or minutes, preferably within a few days. For regular meetings with individual staff members, writing summary notes about the meeting will help you to keep track of each employee's performance. You can follow up on particular issues raised at meetings, note when to revisit a particular topic, and in general keep track of each employee's progress. Notes from meetings can be shared with staff members, to ensure that you and each employee have a shared understanding of the discussions from the meetings. Notes from meetings with staff members can be helpful for performance evaluation purposes, both for noting the accomplishments of a high-performing individual and for generating the paperwork necessary when corrective action must be taken.

For unit or department meetings, minutes help keep all staff, whether or not they attended the meetings, on track and informed. Minutes should include points raised at the meetings, key components of discussions, decisions that were made, decisions that still need to be made, tasks to be performed, staff responsible for these tasks, next steps, and so on. Sample minutes from an executive committee or library management group meeting are shown in figure 11.3. Only action items, decisions, and key updates are included in these minutes. Distributing the meeting minutes promptly is important, both for you as a supervisor, so that you can manage the activities and work of your unit, and for staff members, who may need reminders about the activities taking place in the unit or organization and their own roles in the process. As the supervisor, you are responsible for the necessary follow-up to the meeting. You must make sure that staff understand their responsibilities and carry them out.

Sample Meeting Minutes

Reference Committee Minutes, No. 201
March 16

1. Minutes

The minutes to the March 2 Reference Committee meeting were approved.

2. Library Storage Facility Update

Construction bids for the facility will likely go out mid- to late April.Librarians are working on selection of titles in preparation for closing branch libraries. Initial selections are due May 1.

3. Revised Computer Rotation

Discussed the updated computer rotation schedule for workstations in library.

4. Hours

Library hours were reviewed. Based on usage counts, the current hours schedule will remain effective for the next year.

5. Distribution of Minutes

Committee minutes will be distributed electronically only and posted on the staff intranet.

6. Student Budgets

March 23 is the deadline to report on the status of the student assistant wages budget.

7. Announcements

The next committee meeting will be April 6.

Follow-Up after Meetings

For meetings where your purpose was to gather input or brainstorm ideas, it is critical that you relay to individuals who participated in the meetings the results of the meetings and any decisions made. You should explain why you have decided whatever you decided and why some ideas or suggestions that were raised cannot be implemented at this time. This will help staff to realize that their participation and input are valued and that while you cannot implement all of their ideas all of the time, you appreciate their time, effort, and creativity.

Benefits of Meetings

Meetings provide a mechanism for sharing information, decision making, problem solving, idea generation or brainstorming, and team building, to name just a few of the benefits. With the increasing ease of use of e-mail for communication purposes in libraries, it may be tempting to forgo scheduling at least some meetings with staff. While it is not a good idea to meet just for the sake of meeting, meetings do indicate to your staff that you value their input and contributions to the unit and organization and that you find meeting with them in person to be useful in your management of the unit. Take care to consider carefully whether meeting in person is appropriate and necessary. If there is a clear need, schedule the meeting. If not, an alternative to a group meeting that will take care of the issue may be more appropriate.

Summary

In conclusion, keep in mind the following basic tenets of good meetings.

As the meeting leader, you will do the following:

- Distribute the agenda in advance.
- Set goals and discussion time limits for each agenda item.
- Start on time.
- Stay on task.
- End on time.
- Disseminate minutes in a timely manner.

As the meeting leader, you encourage all participants to do the following:

- Follow agreed-upon meeting guidelines.
- Come to the meeting prepared.
- Remember that only one person speaks at a time.
- Participate but not dominate.
- Expect differences.

- Respect differences.
- Disagree in a respectful manner.

NOTES

1. Myrna J. McCallister and Thomas H. Patterson, "Conducting Effective Meetings," in *Practical Help for New Supervisors*, ed. Joan Giesecke (Chicago: American Library Association, 1997), 58.
2. Joan Giesecke, *Practical Strategies for Library Managers* (Chicago: American Library Association, 2001), 34–35.
3. Barbara I. Dewey and Sheila D. Creth, *Team Power: Making Library Meetings Work* (Chicago: American Library Association, 1993), 28.

Project Management

Chris arrives at work one day to learn that her colleague, the head of collection development, has taken an unexpected leave of absence just as he was ready to head a journal cancellation project. Chris is asked to step in and lead a team to plan and identify 10 percent of the journal collection that can be eliminated in order to balance the budget. The team will have six months to consult with interested groups and identify a clean list of titles that will be canceled. Every department in the library is impacted by this budget problem, from selectors to reference staff to the technical services and information technology staff. How will Chris go about ensuring that all these stakeholders are involved and yet meet the short deadline for this project? Chris could decide to make all the decisions herself, but she knows that will not be effective. For one thing, she is not a subject expert in every area, and she does not know all the intricacies of the various electronic licenses, package plans, and consortium purchases that determine what titles can actually be eliminated. Moreover, this is not the first time the library has had to cancel journals, and she understands that the simpler decisions have already been made. This time, the library will be cutting core titles. What will Chris do? How can she organize this work and meet the deadline? Chris decides to meet with her colleague Jamie to get some ideas on how to proceed. Jamie suggests using project management processes to carry out this assignment. Chris says, "Tell me more. What are project management processes, and how do I use them on this assignment?"

Project Management Overview

The previous scenario is not all that unusual in today's libraries. Supervisors and managers may find themselves called upon to head interdepartmental projects or organization-wide task forces. When these assignments involve a project with a defined beginning and end, you may want to use a formal project management structure to organize and carry out the assignment. Project management is used extensively in the information technology field, where implementing new systems and resolving problems are often done as projects. Using a formal project management process will help you plan, organize, manage, and deliver projects with defined outcomes.[1]

Before you accept the assignment to head a project management work team, you will want to determine if project management is an appropriate process to use to structure the work. Are you being given a true project as the assignment? A project is a planned undertaking and set of related activities that has a defined beginning and end. It is often an interdepartmental undertaking that includes staff and stakeholders that go beyond one department. The scope of the project often impacts many parts of the organization. While you can use a project management process within your department, you may find it most helpful when working between organizational units and on larger projects.

The Players

There will be many people or stakeholders inside and outside of the organization who will be part of a project: top leadership, project sponsor, project manager, project team members, and customers or clients who will be impacted by the results of the project. Each group has a defined role in the process. Management is responsible for identifying projects, assigning priorities to projects, identifying the project manager, and providing ongoing support. At the end of the project, management is responsible for recognizing and rewarding the project manager and team.

The sponsor of the project is the member of the management team who authorizes the project, grants the project manager the authority to complete the project, and supports the project manager throughout the life of the project. The sponsor is responsible for finding the resources needed by the team to accomplish the charge.

The project manager is who heads the project team and controls the processes that make the project happen. The project manager negotiates for time and resources needed by the team. Being a project manager can turn into a full-time job. The project manager needs to negotiate for changes in his or her work assignments in order to be sure that he or she has the time to devote to the project.

The project team consists of the people responsible for doing the work. These people are chosen, based on the skills needed by the team, by the project manager to carry out the charge to the group.

Customers or users are the groups that will in some way be impacted by the outcomes of the project. In the journal cancellation project, users can include the faculty and students in a school or academic environment, the library users in a public setting, or the members of a company for a special library.

As part of the planning process, project team members will want to be sure to identify as many of the stakeholders as they can. This way, the team can be sure that groups who need to be consulted or informed about the project will receive appropriate and timely communication.

Managing the Project Process

There are four phases to a project: initiation, planning, execution, and close-down. It is important to be sure to go through all four phases, including closing down the project, in order to have a successful project.

Project Initiation

In the initial phase of the project, the size, scope, and complexity of the project are identified. As the project manager, you will want to use this time to establish the parameters of the project, choose the project team, and negotiate your authority, your time commitment, and the resources you will have available to you. For your own survival, be sure you negotiate which of your regular responsibilities you will not be fulfilling so that you will have time to devote to the project.

Choosing your project team is a crucial step in creating a successful venture. Work with the sponsor of the project to identify the skills that are needed. Then choose members of the organization who have the skills you need for successful completion. Look for people who can complement your strengths and bring diverse viewpoints and experiences to the effort.

Review the charge to the team with the sponsor. Be sure you understand exactly what is being asked of the group and agree to the outcomes. How will you know if you are successful? For example, with the journal cancellation project, Chris needs to know exactly what journal cost total is 10 percent of the budget. Because journal costs change every year, she must understand how to determine the subscription cost for a given title and ensure that the project sponsor agrees. Clarification on goals for the project is crucial before beginning the project. This will help avoid problems later.

Outline the steps needed to begin the project. Who needs to be contacted as part of the initiation phase? How will Chris report to the sponsor and other members of the management group? How will Chris assign roles to team members? How will Chris work with the sponsor if changes are needed in the project? What type of funding can Chris expect for the project? These are the kinds of questions Chris will want to be sure are answered as part of the initiation phase.

Finally, in this initial stage, Chris will establish how to keep track of the correspondence, activities, and deliverables that are part of the project.

Creating a project notebook, either in print or online, can help Chris keep the group and the procedures organized. It will be important to record decisions made throughout the process, communications sent, and reports submitted. Establishing how to document progress in this project initiation stage will make it easier to keep track of the project throughout the life of the team.

Project Planning

There are six basic steps for planning a project: defining the objectives, structuring the project, scheduling the project, analyzing the plan for risks, reviewing the plan for assumptions, and establishing controls.

Define the objectives. Define the scope of the project. What is the problem to be solved? What are the deliverables for this project and how will they be measured? How will Chris know when the project is finished? These questions need to be answered as a first step in the planning process. In the journal cancellation project, Chris will want to know what needs to be included in the list of journals. Does she need ISSN numbers, costs, publisher information, vendors, or just a list of journal titles? Will the list be in a spreadsheet format, done from an online system, or handwritten? Working out these details now will help ensure that Chris and her team will not need to redo work once it is done.

Structure the project. Now is the time to divide the project into manageable tasks. Identify the tasks to be accomplished and the order in which the tasks will be done. These are known as work breakdown structures and help to develop a logical approach to the work that will need to be done.

Part of the planning process includes developing a communication plan. Often this is the step we are most likely to skip or do quickly. However, having a well-thought-out communication plan can be the difference between successful projects and projects with problems. In the communication plan, include when and how reports on progress will be given and to whom. How will stakeholders be consulted? Will publicity for the project be needed? If so, who will do the publicity and when? In the journal cancellation project, Chris will plan how to announce the project to the constituencies. How will Chris alert users that journals will be canceled? How will Chris keep members of the staff informed of progress so they can answer questions about the project from interested stakeholders? The more Chris communicates and follows a careful plan for communicating, the fewer problems she will have with misinformation and rumors getting out and destroying the progress or Chris's credibility.

Schedule the project. Now that you have identified the tasks, estimate the resources you will need to accomplish those tasks. Resources include staff time as well as budget resources, supplies, and equipment needed for the project. Also identify the amount of time needed for each task. Some tasks may need to be accomplished before others can begin. Others may be done simultaneously. Some tasks may be accomplished more quickly by increasing the resources devoted to the tasks. Identify those tasks that are most critical and be sure you have allowed enough time to accomplish these activities. Get agreement on the budget and timeline from your sponsor or management group.

Assess risks. Now that you have the tasks listed and a schedule in mind, assess the risks involved in the project. What happens if an internal deadline is missed? How likely is it that supplies or equipment could be delayed? How likely is it that the project will result in adverse publicity for the organization? How can you decrease the chances of various problems occurring? Are there things you can do in your plan to decrease any particular risk from becoming a problem?

Review the plan for assumptions. Can the timeline be met? Are the resources you need available? Can the work be done as outlined in the plan? Think about the assumptions you made when developing the task list and be sure those assumptions are still valid.

Establish controls. Negotiate the budget and the plan with management. Review the key statement of work with the sponsor, and be sure that the key stakeholders have a clear understanding of what you plan to do and how you plan to do it. Be sure everyone understands the project size, duration, and outcomes. Finally, determine how you will make changes in the plan as needed and how you will keep the sponsor and management group informed of changes as they occur.

Once you have reviewed and agreed to a plan of action, you are ready to execute the project.

Project Execution

Now is the time to follow your plan. Initiate activities, assign resources, train staff as needed, and make sure that quality measures are being met. You may need to do some team building here to be sure that those involved in the project work well together as a team that is dependent on each member in meeting its assignments.

Monitor progress on each task and be sure your team members are doing the work they said they would do. Continually compare progress on activities to the baseline plan to ensure you are on target. Adjust resource allocations as needed if budgets get ahead or behind schedule. Reassign personnel if needed to meet the project deadlines.

Make changes and adjustments as needed to keep the project on track. You may need to change specifications, internal deadlines, or redo activities if a task gets bungled. Also, identify new activities that may be needed but were not anticipated in the planning process. For example, in the journal cancellation project, Chris may need to add in meetings with interested faculty if she did not include those initially or if faculty become more concerned than anticipated. Finally, decide what to do if an activity is delayed. Can you rearrange tasks, adjust schedules, or move resources to bring the project back on track? Be sure you are maintaining the project workbook and documenting progress throughout.

Project Closedown

You have finished your tasks, met your deadlines, and are ready to end the project. Be sure you formally close down the project so everyone will know that you are done. Notify stakeholders that the project is concluded and deliverables have been finished. Work with management and customers to assess the strengths and weaknesses of the deliverables. Have you provided the final product that was needed? Can the organization use the work you did?

In addition to ending the tasks, you need to close down the team. Assess the team members and support their transitions back to their regular jobs. Finalize documentation and submit any required reports. And, most important, celebrate your success. You have done a great job and deserve to celebrate that success. The celebration is also a way for the organization to thank all of the team members for their help in making the project a success.

Simplified Project Management

The project management process can be simplified to be used to help organize multistep projects. For example, in the scenario of a serials cancellation project, a simplified project management process can be used by technical services to design workflow to cancel the many subscriptions that are being dropped. In order to cancel numerous subscriptions, the technical services unit will have to verify all the titles to be canceled, review and modify the various order and serial records, notify vendors and publishers, and be sure the public catalog accurately reflects the revised holdings for the library. Each of these activities includes a number of steps that must occur, and the steps need to be performed in the correct order for the records to be modified correctly and to avoid duplicate work. These types of projects, with multiple steps and multiple deadlines, lend themselves to a project planning process.

To see how the simplified process can work, let us revisit Jamie and his colleagues in technical services. They face the challenge of determining how best to cancel the journal subscriptions and revise all of the appropriate records so that the library does not pay for titles that it no longer wishes to receive. The head of technical services puts together a small project team to oversee the records project. In the first meeting, the group determines the steps that are needed to verify that the titles can be canceled (i.e., are not part of package plans or multiyear subscriptions), close the order records, revise all related records, and notify the vendors and publishers. For each activity, the group determines who can help with the project, what resources are needed, and what equipment will be needed. The group then sets deadlines based on the timing of invoices. All records need to be revised prior to the receipt of the serial renewal invoices. Using backward planning, the group assigns deadlines to each step to ensure that the project ends on time.

There are other planning techniques that can be used by the group to break down the workflow for the project.[2] Gantt charts provide a graphic way to outline the progress of activities and to avoid overlapping deadlines. The program evaluation and review technique (PERT), or critical path analysis, is a method that helps planners determine the order in which activities need to occur for a project to be successful. Online tools for project management to guide projects through the various stages, such as SharePoint, Zoho, Smartsheet, and WorkZone, to name just a few, are available. Microsoft's Office 365 suite includes Project and Planner, two newer tools for project management. Even relatively simple Excel spreadsheets can help the team keep track of activities, deadlines, and progress on the project.

Once the team outlines the steps in the process and identifies who can help with each step, the planning group notes how the work will be revised and evaluated and how success will be measured. Because a project such as a serials cancellation project could easily involve all members of the technical services departments, including staff who may not have much experience with serial records, the team must remember to include time to train staff to complete the records revision activities.

As the previous discussion shows, taking an organized approach to planning—carefully listing the many activities needed to complete a large project, assigning tasks to individuals, assigning deadlines, ensuring that evaluation occurs throughout the project, and revising plans if needed as the project continues—increases the chances that the project will be completed successfully.

Summary

By following a formal planning and project process, you can manage both large and small projects and bring them to successful outcomes. Skipping steps or cutting short the process will increase the chance of failure. Instead, take the time needed to do the project correctly and thoroughly. In the end, you will save time and resources that would be needed to redo the work. Project management can be very satisfying and fun. When done well, it can help you accomplish complex, interdepartmental tasks and show management that you are a successful project manager.

NOTES

1. Numerous books outline the formal project management process. For an overview of the process, see Patricia Buhler, *Alpha Teach Yourself Management Skills in 24 Hours* (Indianapolis, IN: Alpha Books, 2001), 83–98; and George M. Doss, *IS Project Management Handbook* (New York: Prentice Hall, 2000).
2. Bob Pymm and Damon Hickey, *Learn Library Management*, 2nd ed. (Friendswood, TX: Total Recall, 2007).

PART THREE

Leading Organizations

Communication Skills

Good communication skills are the key to being a successful supervisor and manager because, first and foremost, communication is about establishing and maintaining relationships. As a manager, you are responsible for building your team, establishing a good working relationship with your peers, and developing a positive relationship with your boss. Good communication skills are essential to developing these diverse relationships.

Good communication is about efficiently transmitting your message. How you communicate will set the tone for your unit. If you are clear in your communications, you will create a healthy environment. If you are abrupt and noisy, you will create a stressful environment. If you are always vague and unclear in your

FIGURE 13.1

Communication Model

SOURCE: Joan Giesecke, *Practical Strategies for Library Managers* (Chicago: American Library Association, 2001), 78.

messages, you will set a tone of secrecy and uneasiness and your team members may question your vision for the unit.

At the most basic level, communication involves a message, a sender of the message, a receiver for the message, and feedback about the transmission (see figure 13.1). Communication can be spoken (live and in person or via technology, recorded on a voice mail) or written (formal memo, handwritten note, e-mail, text message, IM, etc.), and it may include a nonverbal component (your physical "presence" in meetings with staff). Regardless of the method or medium, when communication is successful, information is "processed, reviewed, clarified, and revised until both the sender and receiver completely understand each other."[1]

Know Your Audience

With whom do you want to communicate and why? Is the receiver your supervisor, a colleague, someone you supervise, or an external client (a library board member, an upset library patron, a colleague at another library, etc.)? What is the purpose of your message? Do you want to convey to staff a new personnel policy, a request for input on a possible new service, or an announcement of an upcoming meeting? The transmission method and message form will vary depending on what information you need to convey, whether an action or response is necessary, and how quickly action must take place. Our backgrounds, experiences, and personalities affect how we seek and use information. In effective communication, you will want to match the form of the message to the recipient's view of the world. Carl Jung identified four types of people: thinkers who are analytical and work with facts, intuitors who deal in ideas and concepts, sensors who are action oriented, and feelers who are ruled by emotions.[2] Each of these types may hear a given message differently. Sharing lots of ideas with a person who prefers facts and figures will not be very effective. Talking in terms of feelings and values to a person who wants to do something and needs action will also be ineffective. Instead, frame your ideas in data for the thinkers in your unit and in action terms for the sensors. You can then effectively convey the same information to very different recipients.

Other factors, such as the message recipient's age, rank in the library relative to your rank, cultural background, and technological expertise and experience levels, may have a place in both how you deliver a message and how well it is received. Depending on the situation and the people involved, a supervisor may want to use more than one method to communicate the message.

Emergency communication. Chris's town is hit with a major snowstorm on a Friday evening, and the mayor orders all city operations closed until Monday. The library director phones Chris and other supervisors on Friday evening to alert all of them that the library will be closed. Chris immediately contacts weekend staffers, including part-time high school and college student library clerks. She telephones one staffer at home, reaches the Sunday supervisor at his cellphone number, and sends text messages to the part-time clerks. Once she has reached all staff working the weekend shifts, she sends an e-mail message to the departmental e-mail alias, alerting everyone to the details: why the library closed, plans for reopening, where to find updates to the weather situation, and how to handle time cards for scheduled personnel.

Chris manages to reach all affected staff—through the medium most likely to reach them. By having a communication or contact tree in place prior to the weather emergency, she is able to share the news quickly and efficiently, informing those who need to know immediately and providing more detailed information for everyone as well.

New personnel policy on schedule adjustments. Jamie's library administration wants to implement a new policy for scheduling. Jamie's department has had a long history of flexible scheduling, or flextime, and he is concerned about staff reactions. He himself had a flexible schedule before he became a supervisor. This is a big change for Jamie's unit, and Jamie decides that he will need to meet individually with the staff members most affected by the change as soon as possible so that he can answer any questions they may have about their specific situations. Then he will communicate with the entire unit at a staff meeting, or if the timeliness of the announcement is a concern, he will send a detailed e-mail.

As a manager, Jamie balances his responsibilities to implement the new policy with his care for his employees, taking the time to meet with staff individually to alert them to the upcoming changes.

Listening

After planning your message, you can then think about how you will listen for feedback. Active listening skills are crucial for supervisors. Obviously, you want to practice good listening skills when you are the message receiver. First, demonstrate that you are receptive to the message you are about to receive. Acknowledge the sender by nodding and injecting an occasional comment, such as, "Yes" or "Interesting" or "I see." Stay focused on the speaker and the message.

Show interest by listening carefully and attentively. Notice the speaker's emotions as well as the text of the message. Notice if the words match the emotions. If these do not match, take time to ask questions and clarify meaning until you understand how the speaker's emotional state merges with the message.

Be sure you are listening to the speaker rather than framing your response. It can be easy for a busy supervisor, with many demands on his or her time and many tasks to accomplish, to become distracted by other thoughts and not listen carefully. You need to be sure you understand the message before you respond. If you do not listen to and clarify the message being sent before you respond, you may find yourself responding to the wrong message. You will complicate the communication process when you do not practice active-listening skills.

Try, as a receiver of a message, not to make judgments until you have received all the information that the speaker wants to communicate. Try to listen for understanding rather than listening for only agreement. Be open to hearing other ideas even when the ideas are different from yours. If you rush to a judgment or conclusion, you may miss important details or nuances in the message. You may then respond inappropriately and may unnecessarily complicate the communication process.

One way to force yourself to pause before you respond is to silently count off a few seconds before beginning to speak. This brief silence will ensure that the speaker has completely finished his or her thoughts and is not just pausing between points.

Once it is your turn to speak, begin by asking clarifying questions. Also, be sure to briefly summarize the speaker's key points before you frame your response. Only then can you be sure you have accurately heard the speaker's message.

As the sender of a message, you also want to practice active listening. Be sure you hear your receiver's response. Watch for comprehension and understanding. Ask supporting questions and provide additional information if you sense that your message is not being received. By taking time to clarify the major points of your message and to actively listen to responses, you will have a better chance of creating a successful communication encounter.

Reading

One challenge for supervisors is to keep up with all the written material and readings that are part of the job. This material can be in print but increasingly is electronic. Developing an efficient system for handling the reading of materials can make the job much easier.[3] Effective reading means developing a system for quickly scanning material, assessing the importance of the item, and locating the key messages. Keeping print material from accumulating into huge piles and finding a system to organize online communication will help keep you from becoming overwhelmed. Sort items into categories ranging from urgent items you need to read and act upon immediately, to the items you want to read and study in depth, to those you can declare nonessential. For less important items, scan them quickly and move on. Delete them, file them, discard them, or route them as needed, but do get them off your desk and computer. Act upon or write your responses to urgent items as quickly as possible. You want to resolve these issues and keep them moving. For important, in-depth items, set aside time to concentrate on these issues and read the appropriate material. Find a time during your day or week that you can set aside for in-depth study. Use that time to thoroughly read and study the important items that have reached your desk.

By staying on top of your daily mail, both paper and e-mail, responding to urgent items, and taking time to study the truly important material, you can be sure you are not missing key messages in your organization. You will set a good tone for your unit, as issues will not become bogged down because you did not take the time to keep up with your mail and e-mail.

Written Communication

As a supervisor, you will find that you need good written-communication skills. You will be responsible for preparing reports, writing evaluations of your staff, developing policy statements, and communicating with your supervisors and staff. In addition, in today's world of e-mail communication, you will also be writing information to give to your staff that traditionally may have been communicated orally.

Good writing takes practice.[4] Think about the message you want to convey and how you want that message to be delivered. Are you preparing a formal report to be shared with those above you in the organization? Are you sending a procedural change notification to your department? Are you communicating with groups outside of your organization? Each audience is different and has different needs. You want to be sure that your writing style is appropriate for the audience. For example, an academic-style report may be appropriate for a professional journal article but may not be effective for conveying information to your unit. A library-use policy may eventually need several versions, one printed on paper and others for the library's website; the content will be the same, but the arrangement on the paper, screen, and mobile device may need to vary in order to effectively communicate with the different audiences. An informal, chatty memo to your group may be fine to alert them to a minor change in policy. This same style, though, is not appropriate for your annual report. Be sure that your style of writing fits with your audience and with the purpose of your communication.

Next, in preparing to write, you should review or outline the purpose of your communication. What do you want to accomplish with your writing? Do you want to entice the public to a program or convey a policy change? Both actions are important but have very different purposes.

Third, consider the message you want to relay. What are the facts you want to get across to others? What are the key points you want to be sure your audience recognizes in your writing?

Once you have identified your audience, sufficiently outlined your purpose, and decided on your main message, you are ready to begin drafting your piece. Your draft may go through many versions before it is ready. Writing requires effort and editing. It is rare that a person can sit down and compose a memo or a report without needing to make changes and edit the document. Think about the order in which you convey the information. Your primary and important points should appear first. The readers should not have to guess at what you want them to remember. Put the most important message first. Then add in your next most important items, and so on, until you have included all the points you wish to make. Finally, write a concluding paragraph or section to summarize your key points and close your piece.

You will want to review your work and edit the piece to make it as clear as possible. Some word-processing software packages have tools that can help with this, but human review is still recommended. Eliminate any extraneous and unnecessary words. Do not use five words if three will do. Use active sentence structures to maintain clarity.

Check your grammar. Do all your nouns and verbs agree with each other? Have you started a paragraph each time you have a new thought or idea to express? Do you have long sentences that cannot be easily understood? Look at how you can shorten and revise your work to increase clarity and understanding while still conveying all the points that you wish to make.

One helpful hint is to read your writing out loud. How does it sound? Do the words flow easily? Are the ideas clear? Reading your work out loud can help you catch grammatical errors and identify where you have used more words than you need.

Good written communication is a core skill for supervisors. Taking your time and reviewing your work before you distribute it will help you become an effective writer.

E-mail

Some dangers in the world of communication involve the misuse of and mistakes made through e-mail communication.[5] It is too easy, sometimes, to think you can just sit down and compose an e-mail and fire it off without review. Poorly written e-mail messages can be as dangerous for a supervisor as a poorly written report. With e-mail, as with all communication, be sure you practice good etiquette. Be careful with your use of abbreviations. For example, not everyone knows the IM abbreviations that dominate some e-mails. Be sure you explain the abbreviations you do include.

Be thoughtful about when to send an e-mail versus a text message. It makes very little sense to send someone an e-mail or text when you are sitting next to that person and can simply turn and talk to him or her in person. E-mail should not be used as a way to avoid oral communication. You will also want to be careful about to whom you send e-mails and how you reply to messages sent to you. Do not copy everyone imaginable on an e-mail message unless the information is truly needed by everyone in the organization or group. Do not "reply all" on a discussion list message if you are sending a private reply to the sender. Not everyone on the list wants to know about your lunch plans. Keep your business e-mails business oriented and do not confuse business and social communication.

One other trap to avoid with e-mail is the urge to send out an e-mail reply when you are upset or angry. That is not the time to be sending messages, even to close friends, as the message could be forwarded to others. E-mail is not a secure communication channel. Rather, treat it as you would a postcard and assume everyone around will be able to see the message. A list of practices to avoid in your e-mails is provided in figure 13.2.

Here's an example to illustrate the dangers of using the e-mail "reply all" option. The library board decides to postpone the annual fund-raiser this year due to staff shortages. Jamie's unit typically organizes and staffs the fund-raiser, so he lets his unit know and he sends an e-mail to all library staff indicating that the fund-raiser will be postponed this year. A supervisor of another unit, who personally enjoys the fund-raiser and often receives input about it from library patrons and staff, reacts angrily and responds to Jamie's message by questioning Jamie's authority, accidentally copying all staff on his reply. Jamie feels undermined by his colleague; Jamie's colleague is embarrassed by his e-mail gaffe and ultimately apologizes to Jamie; staff members who had initially accepted that the postponement was necessary and unavoidable now experience lowered morale and wonder about the library supervisors' working relationship.

E-mail can be very effective when used correctly. E-mail is an efficient communication medium and can help you inform everyone in a group about a change at the same time. It can also help you document that you have relayed needed information to your group. It can help you send updates and non-time-sensitive information to a large number of people.

FIGURE 13.2
E-mail Don'ts

1. **Don't write what you don't want others to know.**

   Ask yourself: Would I want my boss or my mom to read this message?

2. **Don't e-mail just because it seems easier.**

   An e-mail thread that includes more than three new messages isn't easier—just pick up the phone or visit in person with your coworker.

3. **Don't forget to use the spell-check.**

   E-mail at work is still business communication!

4. **Don't leave people guessing.**

   Address your e-mails to the person by name and close with your name.

5. **Don't make a bad impression.**

   Send well-written, clear, and concise messages; grammar and spelling matter.

6. **Don't forward an e-mail unless necessary.**

   Ask yourself: Should I summarize rather than forward? And don't forward without approval of the original sender (coming back to #1 above).

7. **Don't overload attachments.**

   Make it easy for your readers and their e-mail systems.

8. **Don't add personalized graphics.**

   Back to #3: Work e-mails are business communication.

9. **Don't send flaming e-mails.**

   Take care not to react emotionally. Consider drafting a response but then holding it for a while.

SOURCE: "9 Things to Never Do in E-Mail" by Beverly Davenport Sypher, expert in business communication and associate provost for special initiatives at Purdue University.

As a supervisor, think about what you want to communicate with your writing and then pick the best way to get your ideas across to your audience. Whether you are composing an email message, jotting down a list of bullet points you want to mention at a staff meeting, or writing a formal report, remember to think about your audience, review your purpose, and then outline your message. Finally, edit, edit, edit! A well-written and edited e-mail will help you deliver the kind of message you want to send to your group. A poorly written or repetitive report can just as easily hurt you. Communicating well is an art. Take time as a supervisor to practice the art of good writing each time you write.

Barriers to Communication

Unfortunately, noise in the environment can disrupt the transmission and receipt of the message. Noise can be any sort of disruption to your message. Noise can enter the communication system in a number of ways, including the following:

- Background chatter at meetings, side conversations, and smartphone use can distract participants and prevent clear communication.
- Interruptions can disrupt the speaker and cause you to lose track of the message.
- Too much detail can inhibit effective communication. The message can be lost when too many nonessential details are included.
- Irrelevant messages cause noise in the system. Messages that are not relevant to the receiver are unlikely to be remembered.
- Incomprehensible jargon can also confuse the message or lead to misunderstandings.
- Badly timed messages can also be unproductive. For example, asking for a detailed report on a project just as someone is leaving for the day is not going to be helpful.
- Personal prejudices, stereotyping, and biases can influence how one hears a message.
- Confusing or conflicting body language can disrupt communication.
- The emotional state of the sender or receiver can limit one's ability to send or receive information.

How can you minimize noise in your communication? Carefully planning your communication can make the difference between effective communication and noise pollution. Remember, "effective communication is primarily the speaker's responsibility."[6] Be sure you are being honest, open, and clear in your communication. You don't want the receiver of your message to have to read between the lines and guess at your meaning and intent. Be alert to signals from the receiver of the message that you are being unclear. Look for both verbal and nonverbal clues that can tell you if your message has been accurately received. Think about the purpose of your message and what you want to accomplish. Do you need someone to take action? If so, be sure you plan your message so that the action you want taken is clearly stated. Think about the recipients. How much information do they need? Is this an informed audience or one with limited knowledge of your subject? Plan your communication so you link the audience and the message. Be sure the subject of your message is clear and easily identified. Obscurity and ambiguity will only create confusion. Focus and clarity will help ensure that you get the results you want from your message.

Your Reputation and Communication

As a supervisor, you will find that your "reputation, credibility, and intention" impact how effective you can be as a communicator.[7] If staff perception is that you are an honest, straightforward manager who can be trusted, people are more likely to accept your communication at face value. They will not look for hidden meanings and devious messages. Rather, they will be open to communication from you and will try to understand what you are trying to say. If people see you as a supervisor who hides information, they will be more suspicious of communication from you. They will be more likely to look for hidden meanings and hidden agendas. Even when you are being open and honest, the staff may be wary of your communication and may be cautious in accepting information from you. As a manager, your actions will speak louder than words, to quote an old cliché. In communication, as in other areas of management, you will be successful if you think about what you want to accomplish, work with your staff to be clear about your intentions, and be open to communicating and receiving information.

Summary

Good communication skills take practice to develop. Be sure you take time to learn to speak clearly, listen attentively, and respond appropriately. Be an effective communicator by using the following general communication strategies.

Oral communication. Plan your communication carefully. Know what the key points are that you wish to convey. Limit how many points you make at any given time to the amount of information people can absorb. Providing more information than anyone can possibly comprehend in one session is not going to help you communicate your ideas.

Speak clearly and distinctly. Pause frequently and ask for questions to be sure your listeners are following your points. Allow time for questions to be asked.

Summarize your key points or actions to be taken to be sure your listeners remember the points you want to convey.

Practice active-listening skills by paying attention to the speaker, clarifying the message before you speak, and taking time to be sure the speaker has finished before you begin to respond.

Written communication. If you are unsure about your writing skills, then take time to learn to write by writing. Practice your writing skills every day. Read other people's reports and analyze the writing style. What aspects of the report are clear to you? Are there sections that do not make sense? By analyzing others' writing, you can begin to identify what makes writing successful and what does not. As you practice writing, use the following rules to help simplify your writing style.

1. Talk about it first. Know what you want to say before you start to write.

2. Talk to the reader on paper. Pretend the recipient of your letter is sitting across the table from you. Write your report or letter as if you were talking to this person.

3. Write to express, not impress. Write for understanding. Do not use long sentences when shorter sentences will do. Do not use so many big words that your audience cannot follow your meaning.

4. Short is better. Write enough to be clear and then stop.

5. Say it first and last. Put your purpose in your first sentence and summarize it in your last sentence.

6. Read for meaning, not glory. Reread your writing from the reader's point of view. Be sure your audience will understand your message rather than worrying about how to make yourself look good.

7. Do not strive for perfection. There is no such thing as the perfect report. Once your piece is understandable and well organized, let it go. You have other things to do besides re-editing every single document you produce.[8]

Good communication skills come with practice. Good communication skills help you create positive working relationships with your staff, your peers, and your supervisor and will help lead to success in your role as a library leader.

NOTES

1. William A. Salmon, *The New Supervisor's Survival Manual* (New York: AMACOM, 1999), 93.
2. Cited in Arthur Young, *The Manager's Handbook: The Practical Guide to Successful Management* (New York: Crown, 1986), 135.
3. Ibid., 138.
4. Ibid., 136–37.
5. Gary McClain and Deborah S. Romaine, *Everything Managing People Book* (Avon, MA: Adams Media, 2002), 165–66.
6. Salmon, *The New Supervisor's Survival Manual*, 97.
7. Ibid.
8. Young, *The Manager's Handbook*, 143; McClain and Romaine, *Everything Managing People Book*, 164–65.

Organizational Climate and the Art of Motivation

As a supervisor, you are primarily responsible for the organizational climate of your unit. You may not realize that you have great influence over how your staff will view the unit and the organization. If you are positive and inclusive in your approach, you can create an environment where employees feel their work matters and the organization cares about them. If you see the organization in "us versus them" terms, your unit will see enemies throughout the organization. If you are passionate about the mission of the organization, you can create an atmosphere of excitement that keeps your unit motivated, even in tough times.

One challenge you face in creating a good climate, though, is to learn how to recognize what kind of environment exists in your unit and organization and to improve the environment if it is not as positive as you would like it to be. There are many ways to describe organizational climates. This chapter looks at two approaches to describing the climate in your unit and examines ways to improve that climate.

Character of the Organization

One way to describe the climate in an organization is to look at the character of the organization. How can you describe an organization in terms of character? William Bridges, in his book *The Character of Organizations*, presents a system for using the Myers-Briggs Type Indicator (MBTI) as a way to look at the character of an organization and the type of climate that character type creates.[1] While the MBTI has been used less often by organizations in the past decade, Bridges's system gives supervisors a different way to think about the unit and about how to develop the unit to be successful. Based on the theories of Carl Jung, Bridges examines four aspects of personality to describe how a person focuses attention, gathers information, makes decisions, and generally deals with the world.[2]

Focusing attention

Extroversion—relates more to the outer world of people

Introversion—relates more to the inner world of ideas

Gathering information

Sensing—works with facts

Intuition—looks for possibilities and relationships

Making decisions

Thinking—makes decisions based on impersonal analysis and logic

Feeling—makes decisions based on personal values

Lifestyle

Judging—prefers a planned, orderly life

Perceiving—prefers a flexible, spontaneous, open life

In the workplace, these aspects of personality may provide clues to how people will likely relate to work groups, decision making, and problem-solving activities. Understanding these relationships can help supervisors understand their units.

William Bridges has taken the four broad categories and created a way to look at the overall character of the unit. He looks at the organization's approach to its customers, how the organization gathers information and makes decisions, and how quickly the organization takes action. These four categories create a vocabulary for talking about the organization or unit.[3]

Focus or orientation of the unit

Extroversion—outward-looking to the market to determine what direction to take

Introversion—inward-looking to the organization's own technical abilities and leaders' ideas to solve problems and set direction

Gathering information

Sensing—looks at facts, current realities, and details of a situation

Intuition—looks at the big picture rather than the details

Making decisions

Thinking—impersonal decision making, based on principles

Feeling—more value-driven decision making with a personal component

Dealing with the world

Judging—tends to make decisions quickly

Perceiving—tends to keep options open

Each of these characteristics will yield different climates and different ways of operating. Understanding the different orientations and approaches that work in the organization can help you build a successful unit.

How can you determine the character of your organization? Climate surveys, such as the one Bridges includes in his book, are available for groups to take.[4] If your organization has funds for professional development or organizational development, consider purchasing an inventory or survey for your unit or department. Once you and your staff have completed a survey instrument or inventory, you will want to discuss the results with your unit. The results may help you identify the major characteristics of your organization. You can discuss how well the results describe what you already know about the organization. You can also use these discussions as opportunities to talk about how you want to function as a unit, what strengths you want to highlight, and what challenges you face as a group working within the larger organization. As a supervisor, you may find that the conversations about the organization are more important than the results of the survey. By discussing how you want to operate as a unit, you will be better able to build a working climate that is successful for the unit and the organization.

How else can you use these ideas to your advantage? In addition to using survey results as a way to begin a conversation about the unit, you can also use what you've learned about your unit's culture to create and implement new programs and services. By knowing how to bring about change, you can create a working environment that is geared toward success. For example, if you and your unit wish to implement a new chat service or other new service, you will want to tailor the proposal to match the characteristics of the organization. For example, following Bridges's model, if your organization is basically an extroverted one that looks outward for ideas, then you will want to survey organizations that already have implemented the new reference service and describe their experiences in your proposal. If your organization is more introverted and inward-looking when seeking advice, then you may want to ask the reference service experts in your organization to review your unit's proposal and help tailor your ideas to match the organization.

If your organization is more comfortable with facts and details, then be sure to include relevant facts and details in your proposal. For a chat reference service, include an analysis of the software used for the service, describe how reference shifts might be scheduled, and include details on the resources needed to implement the service. If, on the other hand, your organization concentrates on the big-picture idea, emphasize how chat reference fits into the overall service delivery program. Describe how the new service will enhance the work of the organization. While you still need to include details on the software to be used and how you propose to incorporate the new service into your existing structure, you will want to be more succinct and less detail oriented in an intuitive organization than in a sensing organization.

By understanding the overall character of the organization, you can help employees in your unit make sure that the work they do is presented in ways that will be successful in the organization. Your unit's ideas will be more likely to succeed. Your unit will be better able to contribute positively to the work of the organization. Members of your unit are less likely to become disillusioned with the organization when they can see their ideas having an impact on their work. Then you will have created a positive and successful climate for your unit.

Creating a Professional Environment

As a supervisor and manager, you will also be responsible for creating and maintaining the professional environment of your unit. Your unit's success within the larger library organization will depend on the leadership you provide in this area. The first impressions we leave with library users, library board members, and our colleagues in other units are very important. Some libraries have policies in place that help manage these first impressions. Examples include policies or practices about name tags, customer service, and dress codes. If your library has policies like this, you can set a good example and help your staff to understand and follow the policies. If your library or larger organization does not have policies like these, you may want to consider adopting them for your unit. This is a good time to check in with your supervisor colleagues to see if they would also like to enact policies around creating a professional environment. Working together you can enact this change in your library organization.

Creating an Inclusive, Positive Climate

Another way to look at the organizational climate is to determine how inclusive the climate is for the diverse individuals in your unit. In an inclusive environment, differences among staff are recognized as strengths you can build on in the organization. Blending and integrating those strengths will create a positive working environment where staff are inspired to do their best work. You can create an inclusive environment by building trust among the members of your unit, by treating everyone with respect, and by promoting good communication.

Trust. Trust develops when staff feel they are treated fairly and as individuals. In a unit with a high level of trust, rewards are the result of effort, not favoritism. Employees must know that if they perform at the required level, you will follow through with a reward that they value.[5] Staff must feel that their views are appreciated and their input is gathered and used. Office politics are kept to a minimum. Decision making is transparent, and staff can see the connection between input, decision making, and results.

Respect. Respect is another key element in creating a positive working environment. Again, when staff feel they are recognized as individuals, when their ideas are taken seriously, and when they feel their contributions are important, they will feel respected. If staff feel they are being treated as interchangeable parts, they may feel taken for granted and will not see the workplace as a positive environment.

Communication. Enough cannot be said about how important good communication is for creating a positive working environment. Good communication is a two-way process. In a positive environment, staff feel they are aware of what is going on in the unit and organization. They also feel their input is sought and used in making the unit a success. Feeling "in the know" is a major motivator to many staff and helps them understand how they can best contribute to the unit and organization. Staff want to be part of a successful organization. Good communication is a key part of helping staff know how they can contribute to, participate in, and benefit from working in the unit and organization.

Steps to Inclusion

What specifically, then, can you do as a supervisor to create a positive, inclusive working climate?

First, be sure you set the right tone for the office. You must understand, embrace, and utilize diversity in the unit and accept the diverse contributions each individual makes to the unit. Always be respectful to staff members and signal that you do not tolerate disrespectful behavior from others. For example, do not tolerate inappropriate jokes, humor, or microaggressions. Caution staff who make inappropriate remarks about others that they must stop. If the behavior does not stop, you need to take appropriate disciplinary action. Ignoring inappropriate behavior will create a negative environment for your unit and could result in legal action.

Share information with everyone in the unit, and be sure individuals are not left out of the communication loop. You need to ask for input and use that input or explain why you cannot use input you received. In other words, make it clear to staff how you made a decision and how you used their ideas.

Give credit to others for their work and ideas. You will quickly lose your staff's trust and respect if you take credit for and are rewarded for their ideas.

Finally, practice listening to your staff. One of the hardest things to do as a supervisor is to really listen to ideas that run counter to what you believe and to try to find positive aspects in ideas that may not fit with your view of the unit. Even though it may be difficult to examine others' ideas, it is important to keep an open mind and explore alternative opinions. To quote Amy Poehler, actress and founder of Amy Poehler's Smart Girls website (https://amysmartgirls.com), "if you can speak about what you care about to a person you disagree with, without denigrating or insulting them, then you may actually be heard."[6] By doing so, you will see a broader view of an issue, explore new approaches, and expand your own understanding of an issue. By carefully listening to others and exploring views that do not match your own, you will help your staff members realize that their ideas are valued and, therefore, that they are valued as individuals and as part of the unit. When you do this successfully, staff will model your behavior when interacting with one another and colleagues throughout the organization. For example, when talking with your unit about a new service, ask your staff for ideas and keep track of the many viewpoints expressed. Then summarize those ideas for the unit in order to let staff know that you heard and considered their ideas. Staff can express different viewpoints on scheduling desk shifts, for instance, from how long a shift should be to how many shifts each person should work. By sharing the diversity of viewpoints, the staff will know that they have been heard and will realize that there are many ways to set up the service. Understanding different points of view will make it more likely that staff will understand why all their ideas cannot be implemented.

When you can create an environment where staff are proud of what they do and feel a part of the mission of the organization, you will have the foundation for a very productive unit that can achieve excellence.

Individual Motivation

Once you have looked at the overall climate for your unit and at how you can make that climate as positive as possible, you will want to look at how to inspire each staff member to do the best he or she can do. As a supervisor, you are responsible for creating an environment where employees are motivated to do their best work. To succeed in creating a good working environment, you need to know what motivates your staff and how you can help them want to be productive.

Motivation can be defined as giving someone an incentive to act or giving someone a reason to do something. Motivation is also creating a feeling of enthusiasm or interest that makes someone want to do something. So the supervisor does not motivate someone but rather creates an incentive for action. Motivation itself is self-directed. Either a staff member will want to accomplish a task well or he or she will not. As a supervisor, you want to create the best incentives you can to encourage staff to accomplish the work that needs to be done.

Theories of Motivation

What makes people want to act? In the early twentieth century, researchers studied leadership styles and motivation. Douglas McGregor defined two basic approaches to management known as Theory X and Theory Y.[7] In Theory X, managers believe that most people do not want to work. Therefore, in order to have a productive workplace, supervisors must carefully monitor the work of the employees. Supervisors create detailed rules and procedures for staff to follow so that there is no uncertainty about what is expected or how the work is to be performed. Supervisors assume staff are lazy and will put forth the least amount of effort to get by. These supervisors create an environment that does not foster creativity, is very rule bound, and in which staff have little or no say about how the work is performed. In Theory X, the motivating factor for staff is a paycheck. On the other hand, Theory Y managers believe people want to do a good job. These managers want to create a nurturing environment where staff can be creative and contribute to the organization. Employees in Theory Y want to be useful and productive. Their motivation is the reward of a job well done.

These two views of staff motivation create two very different workplaces. In Theory X, rules and procedures are crucial, and following the rules is the key to success. In Theory Y, staff involvement in the organization and participation in decision making lead to a productive environment. Theories X and Y illustrate how the principles of motivation that we follow impact the types of workplaces we create.

Another major motivation theorist was Abraham Maslow. Maslow looked at human behavior and theorized that people are driven by a hierarchy of needs.[8] First, people want to satisfy their need for food and shelter. Next, they will look for safety and security. Once these basic needs are fulfilled, people will try to satisfy their need for social affiliation or belonging to a group. Next, people look to fulfill their needs for self-esteem and to feel important and accepted as individuals. Finally, people have a need for self-actualization and thus seek continued growth and development. In Maslow's theory, people do not have to completely satisfy one need before moving on to the next. They may work on more than one need at a time. Still, unless the basic needs are fulfilled at a minimal level, people will not be thinking about higher-level needs such as group belongingness and individual accomplishments. For a supervisor, then, if staff cannot make ends meet on the salaries they receive, they are first going to be motivated to find additional sources of income. Either they will change jobs or they will find second jobs to provide adequate income to meet their needs for food, shelter, and safety. Providing training so a person can learn about himself or herself as an individual will not be effective if you cannot meet that person's basic needs. Maslow's theory helps you as a manager to recognize that the basic resources must be in place before managers can move on to meeting higher-level needs.

Frederick Herzberg took a different approach to motivation. He theorized that there are two basic sets of motivators: those factors that are positive motivators are called satisfiers, and those factors that are negative motivators are called dissatisfiers. Positive motivators include such things as recognition, the work itself, increasing levels of responsibility, and advancement opportunities. Dissatisfiers or negative motivators are factors such as salaries, policies, type of supervision, and working conditions.[9] These negative factors can lead to poor motivation but they do not lead to positive actions. That is, these factors may make people leave an organization but they will not necessarily keep someone working in your organization.

Management theorists began to address the question of what motivates people in the 1950s with the human relations school of management thought. Theorists looked at individual behavior and developed theories to explain why people act in certain ways. These theories identify for supervisors what factors they need to consider in creating a motivating work climate.

While theories of motivation are useful and can help you as a supervisor understand why one way of motivating staff will not work for everyone, the theories do not necessarily offer practical suggestions for how to create an environment where staff are motivated to do their best.

More recently, another theory on motivation, developed by the Gallup Organization and reported in the book *First, Break All the Rules*, offers a more practical approach to motivation.[10] Gallup surveyed over one million individuals to identify those factors that separate organizations or units that are excellent performers from those that are only good.[11] They found that four factors can be used by managers to determine how to create an environment that is motivating to employees:

1. Basic resources to do the job

2. Individual needs

3. Social needs

4. Growth opportunities

Gallup isolated twelve questions that can be used to measure how well individuals believe that the organization is meeting their needs. These twelve questions can then be used to distinguish those environments that lead to high performance from those that do not. The questions are rated on a scale from 1 to 5 where 5 is "strongly agree" and 1 is "strongly disagree." In excellent organizations, employees will answer "5" to all of these twelve questions:

1. I know what is expected from me at work.

2. I have the equipment and materials I need.

3. I have the opportunity to do what I do best each day.

4. Someone at work cares about me as a person.

5. In the last seven days, I have received praise for doing good work.

6. Someone at work encourages my development.

7. The mission or purpose of the company makes me feel my job is important.

8. My fellow employees are committed to doing quality work.

9. At work, my opinion seems to count.

10. I have a best friend at work.

11. In the past six months, someone has talked to me about my progress.

12. In the past year, I have had the opportunity at work to learn and to grow.[12]

These questions identify factors that are similar to Maslow's hierarchy of needs. However, the order for the questions is slightly different. According to Gallup:

> First, employees want to know what they can get from the organization. The first two questions will indicate if employees' basic needs are being met. They are the organizational equivalent of safety and security needs.

> Next, employees want to know what they can give to the organization, and questions 3 through 6 look at these factors. These are equivalent to Maslow's individual needs.

FIGURE 14.1
Theories of Motivation

MASLOW'S HIERARCHY OF NEEDS	HERZBERG'S CONCEPT	ORGANIZATIONAL FOCUS	GALLUP'S QUESTIONS HIERARCHY	ORGANIZATIONAL FOCUS
Safety and security	Dissatisfiers	Basic requirements	Expectations and resources (Q 1-2)	Basic requirements
Social needs	Satisfiers	Contribute to the organization	Individual and self-esteem (Q 3-6)	Individual success
Individual needs	Satisfiers	Individual success	Unit focus (Q 7-10)	Contribute to the organization
Self-actualization	Satisfiers	Growth	Growth and development (Q 11-12)	Growth

Third, employees will want to figure out if they belong in the organization, and questions 7 through 10 examine this issue. Here is where we find Maslow's social needs.

Finally, employees want to know if they can grow in the position, and the last two questions look at this point. Here are Maslow's self-actualization needs.

Gallup has found that by reversing Maslow's individual and social needs, they are better able to identify excellence in the organization. The motivational theories of Maslow, Herzberg, and the Gallup Organization are compared in figure 14.1.

Motivational Factors and the Workplace

Gallup's questions provide a very practical way for managers to look at the environment they are creating in the workplace and examine what they need to do to move their unit to excellence.

Clarifying Expectations and Providing Resources

Managers should first be sure that they have been clear about their expectations. Have you met with each employee and reviewed the expectations for his or her position? Are the expectations included in job descriptions and performance evaluations? Employees should not have to guess at what is expected of them. The supervisor should be able to clarify this information for each position.

Supervisors are also responsible for ensuring that employees have the resources they need to do their jobs. Staff find it very hard to be motivated when basic equipment and supplies are not available. Employees with inadequate equipment will underperform and will lose interest in the organization. No matter how many incentives a manager creates for his or her employees, if employees are scrambling to find supplies and resources, they will not be spending time improving performance.

Identifying Individual Needs

Once the basics are in place, supervisors should talk to each employee about what the employee feels he or she does best and how that can be a part of his or her position or tasks. If someone's talents do not fit the job very well, that employee may be in the wrong position. While he or she may be a good performer, the employee will not achieve excellence when unable to do what he or she does best. Employees also want to know that someone cares about them and that they receive recognition for their work. Acknowledging good performance, encouraging staff, and letting staff know you are concerned about them as individuals will go a long way toward creating a motivating environment.

As you are discussing each person's individual talents and ambitions, you will want to identify specific factors that help each person feel motivated to do a good job. Standard motivators include a sense of achievement, a sense of power, a sense of belonging, and a sense of independence. As you talk to your staff, find out which of these needs are most important to them.[13]

To determine if an employee is motivated by achievement, try to understand if he or she is goal driven. Does the person like to work on projects? Is learning new skills important to him or her? If so, the employee is likely to be looking for ways to be productive and reach new goals. Provide new challenges for this individual. Include both short-term and long-term goals so the person can see that he or she is accomplishing tasks as a long-term project develops.

A person who likes to exert influence and attract attention is likely to be motivated by feeling in control and feeling powerful. These staff can be a challenge when they seek center stage and try to dominate conversations. Enable these staff to contribute positively to the organization by helping them to become in-house experts. Channel their energy into projects where they can express their opinions and be seen as important members of the group.

For an employee who needs to feel a sense of belonging, you will want to be sure he or she has numerous opportunities to interact with colleagues. This person does not necessarily work well alone. Instead, find projects that require a group effort. These staff may also be the social organizers for the unit. Let them plan group events, staff luncheons, and other social opportunities. They will enjoy the opportunity to work with others and provide a positive social environment for the unit.

To determine if an employee is motivated by independence, see if he or she questions procedures and policies that limit the individual's ability to decide how to carry out a task. You will want to be careful not to micromanage these staff. Instead, find ways they can determine their own way of achieving agreed-upon results. Of course, you will want to guard against giving such a staff member so much freedom that he or she does not follow important rules, ignores legal requirements, or refuses to work cooperatively with others.

Contributing to the Organization

After examining how to meet individual needs, it is time to look at how each person can contribute to the organization. Help employees see how the mission of the organization relates to their individual tasks. Talk to people about how they make a difference. Explain to the staff or students who shelve books how they make it possible for library users or other students to more easily find materials when they take time to shelve materials correctly. Show cataloging staff how the work they do makes it possible for patrons to more easily identify needed materials. Each job in the organization is important, and as a supervisor and manager, you should be able to show how each position helps the organization reach its goals.

Supervisors should also be sure they are listening to staff and asking for input as appropriate. Staff will often have the best ideas on how to improve workflow and work procedures. After all, they are the ones doing the work. As supervisors, we cannot be afraid to learn from our employees. Listening to staff is also a way that a supervisor can show respect for employees. Checking your smartphone and reading or answering e-mail while listening to staff ideas will signal that you are not listening and that you do not care. When staff feel that you do not care about them as individuals, they will be less motivated to contribute to the organization.

Job Growth and Development

Finally, help people grow in their jobs. Staff do want to learn and to be challenged to improve. Motivated staff will seek out opportunities to try new things, to enhance their own skills, and to improve in their positions. As a manager, you can encourage such activities and reward people for their successes. Supervisors should talk to their staff about the progress they are making. Gallup has found that having a progress conversation at least once every six months will help staff know how they are doing.[14] These people will stay motivated to excel. A regular progress conversation, or check-in, can be an effective part of the overall performance management cycle.

● ● ● ● ●

When you have created a positive working climate, you will have motivated staff who are inspired to do their best. Creating that climate, though, will take work as you learn how to successfully address the needs of the individuals in your unit while understanding the overall organizational environment. When you can match individual needs with organizational goals, you will have a motivated staff. When you ignore individual differences and try to impose one supervisory approach on all your employees, you will leave some of your staff unmotivated and uninspired. Although it takes time to find the right combination of strategies for each person, the time will be well spent, as you will be rewarded with a well-functioning and productive unit. You will have staff who want to work and who want to make the unit successful.

Summary

Motivation comes from within. You cannot motivate someone to work. You can, however, create an environment where staff are self-motivated to succeed.

Begin by analyzing the overall climate and character of your organization. Determine what strategies will be most successful within the overall climate of the organization.

Once you understand the overall climate of the organization, analyze the climate in your unit. Look for ways to create an inclusive climate that capitalizes on each person's strengths.

Determine the best way to create a motivating climate for each member of your staff. Talk to your staff about their needs. Adjust your style to address the needs of each person. Of course, you need to be sure that you are working within the overall character of the organization.

Regardless of which motivational theory you follow, or what set of advice you prefer, you will be most successful when you truly listen to your staff, understand each person's needs, help staff to hear and understand one another, and match each person's needs with the tasks and projects within the unit.

NOTES

1. William Bridges, *The Character of Organizations: Using Personality Type in Organization Development* (Palo Alto, CA: Consulting Psychologists, 1992), 2.
2. Cited in Kent Hendrickson and Joan R. Giesecke, "Myers-Briggs Type Indicator Profile and the Organization," *Library Administration and Management* 8, no. 4 (Fall 1994): 218–19.
3. Bridges, *The Character of Organizations*, 2–3.
4. Ibid., 115–19.
5. Patricia Buhler, *Alpha Teach Yourself Management Skills in 24 Hours* (Indianapolis, IN: Alpha Books, 2001), 166.
6. Vi-An Nguyen, "Happy Birthday, Amy Poehler! Her 20 Funniest—and Wisest— Quotes," *Parade*, September 16, 2014, http://parade.com/339530/viannguyen/happy -birthday-amy-poehler-her-20-funniest-and-wisest-quotes.
7. Cited in Buhler, *Alpha Teach Yourself Management Skills*, 162–63.
8. Cited in Joan Giesecke, *Practical Strategies for Library Managers* (Chicago: American Library Association, 2001), 44–46.
9. Frederick Herzberg, "One More Time: How Do You Motivate Employees?," *Harvard Business Review* 46, no. 1 (January–February 1968): 53–62.
10. Marcus Buckingham and Curt Coffman, *First, Break All the Rules: What the World's Greatest Managers Do Differently* (New York: Simon and Schuster, 1999).
11. Ibid., 11.
12. Ibid., 43–45.
13. Morey Stettner, *Skills for New Managers* (New York: McGraw-Hill, 2000), 74.
14. Buckingham and Coffman, *First, Break All the Rules*.

Inclusiveness and Diversity

Chris is in her office when Nicole comes in and closes the door. Nicole is a newly hired librarian who is working with the multicultural program. Nicole is concerned that she is being asked to serve on numerous committees and feels that some committees are asking her to serve only because of her ethnicity. She is frustrated because if she accepts all these committee appointments, she won't have time to work with others on important multicultural issues. Nicole tells Chris that if she can't find a way to do the job she was hired to do, she will need to find a new position. Chris takes a moment to collect her thoughts. Chris is now faced with the problem of retaining an important member of her team and fulfilling the library's commitment to diversity. After a moment, Chris comes up with a plan.

Chris suggests that she and Nicole review all the committee assignments and pick only those assignments that are core to Nicole's job. She says that then they will review Nicole's workload and set priorities so Nicole will be able to complete her most important tasks. Nicole isn't convinced that this is a good plan. She feels bad that she will be saying no to committees that need to benefit from diversity. She feels a strong obligation to represent people of color in the library and on the campus. Chris realizes she needs to keep Nicole engaged with the external community in a more focused way to be more effective. Chris then suggests to Nicole that in looking at committee assignments, they pick those where Nicole can make the most difference as a person of color, and she asks Nicole if it would help to meet with others in the community to talk about how to balance committee assignments across the campus to ensure that all voices are heard.

This chapter broadly defines diversity to include culture, gender, LGBTQ, and individuals with disabilities. The benefits of building an inclusive and diverse workforce, opportunities and challenges for supervisors, and how to recognize strengths and capitalize on differences in your employees are discussed.

Defining Diversity and Inclusion

At the most basic level, diversity is the existence and recognition of differences. These differences may be related to ethnicity, nationality, race, gender, age, socioeconomic status, physical disabilities, religious beliefs, political beliefs, sexual orientation, and life experience.

Janice Joplin and Catherine Daus state, "Diversity encompasses any characteristic used to differentiate one person from others."[1] Inclusion is when all individuals are involved and empowered, feel a sense of belonging, and are respected for their beliefs and backgrounds. In other words, diversity is being invited to the party and inclusion is being asked to dance. In late 2015, *Forbes* magazine described diversity and inclusion as a top priority for businesses in 2016 and noted research documenting that gender-diverse companies are 15 percent more likely to outperform their peers, ethnically diverse companies are 35 percent more likely to do the same, and inclusive teams outperform their peers by 80 percent in team-based assessments.[2] Building on this definition, managing and promoting inclusiveness and diversity means taking advantage of the diversity in the workplace to build a stronger

organization. When we value diversity, we can "solve problems using multiple perspectives, relate to customers in their native language and culture,
[and] improve communication."[3]

The US Census Bureau projects that the United States will become more
diverse in coming years, and by 2060, the non-Hispanic population will be
just 44 percent of the total US population.[4] The recruitment and retention of a
diverse workforce, while an important issue for libraries during the past few
decades, is now more crucial than ever. The makeup of the library workforce
must change, with a significant increase in the hiring and retention of staff
from currently underrepresented groups, to best serve students, faculty, and
communities.

The Diverse Workforce

A library (or any organization) with a diverse workforce, with individuals
willing to share new ideas based on their backgrounds and experiences,
will be in a better position to meet the needs of our changing user populations. Better problem solving and increased creativity and innovation are the
results of well-managed diversity in an organization.[5] A culturally diverse
library staff brings different perspectives to library work, which traditionally,
at least in the United States, has had an Anglo-European cultural context.
Many libraries have developed diversity plans to help guide their work in
this area. Consult with your library administration to see if your library has
such a plan.

As a supervisor, you have an important opportunity to help create an
inclusive culture in your unit, as well as a unit with staff members who have
an appreciation of and respect for diversity. Your unit will move forward to
meet organization goals more fully by promoting acceptance of and respect
for different people, ideas, and opinions. Recognizing privilege, as well as
differences in backgrounds, experiences, learning styles, and communication
styles, will enable you to work most effectively with the staff members you
supervise.[6]

Cultural Differences

Mainstream American culture has been heavily influenced by white/Anglo
cultural norms. Creating an environment that welcomes, values, and respects
all members requires developing an understanding of cultural differences

and a realization that not all members of a particular culture will exhibit the same traits or behaviors. For example, researchers have studied variations in preferred learning styles for Native Americans, Hispanic Americans, African Americans, Asian Americans, and European Americans, and while there may be some variances based on cultural experiences, it is crucial to not make assumptions or stereotype but instead to consider each individual's particular style.[7] As a supervisor, you will want to consider learning style preferences when you are training new employees and providing development opportunities for current staff. You will want to invest in training for your team on unconscious bias and structural bias and integrate diversity and inclusion strategies into your hiring practices, retention strategies, performance management systems, and leadership development and training.

Gender Differences

Even though in the United States we have made some strides in achieving gender equity, the 2016 presidential election indicates that we still have work to do. Understanding gender, gender differences, and the complexity of the gender continuum, without stereotyping employees, is still important today. Libraries traditionally employ more females than males, although upper-level management positions in libraries continue to include a disproportionate number of males. Gender differences may account for many of the communication issues that arise in libraries. Compounded by generational differences and cultural differences, gender differences may have major implications for supervisors.

Individuals bring different strengths to the workplace. Research studies and popular literature suggest that boys tend to play in hierarchical groups, with one boy acting as leader, giving orders, and telling others what to do. Boys play games with winners and losers and elaborate systems of rules. In contrast, girls play in small social groups that are inclusive within the group. Their games do not necessarily have winners and losers. Girls are more concerned with being liked than with attaining status within the group.[8]

In the workplace, this behavior pattern continues. For men, conversations are negotiations, with the goal being to achieve and maintain the upper hand; for women, conversations are also negotiations, but the goal instead is to attain closeness, to gain or receive support, and to reach consensus.[9] Generally, men are more likely to be directive, to tell others what to do; resent interruptions; and value completion of tasks and goals. Women tend to work at a steady pace; not consider interruptions as a problem; prefer face-to-face or group interaction over written, impersonal communication; and maintain a complex set of relationships. Men may seem to be more task focused, while women are more relationship focused.[10]

These are generalizations, and while they do not take into account the more recent discussions around transgender staff and individual identification on the gender continuum, they may help you, as a supervisor, understand or interpret behavior that is different from your own. As a supervisor, however, you will want to be sure you are not seeing your employees as categories or stereotypes. Use the research that helps explain gender differences to understand how to adapt your style to be more effective. You want to capitalize on each person's strengths, not discount someone based on an arbitrary category.

Chris manages a large department with ten librarians and staff. She wants the group to function well together, but she recognizes that much of the work involves individuals assisting library users with reference questions, either online during chat reference or in individual sessions with library users. The previous manager, Chris's predecessor, often seemed to apply gender stereotypes in the department. He usually asked the women to arrange all departmental social functions and to pitch in when others were on leave. He expected men to work later shifts so the women could be home early to meet their children after school. He also assumed the female librarians would room together at conferences and allocated less travel funding to them than to the male librarians. Chris needs to be sure she is careful to apply the same policies to everyone and to expect the same level of cooperation from all employees, regardless of gender.

Chris can do a lot to promote harmony in the unit by recognizing different approaches and styles and using those differences to bring multiple perspectives to the unit's work.

LGBTQ Employees

Lesbian, gay, bisexual, transgender, and queer (LGBTQ) staff members deserve a safe working environment where all employees are treated with respect, regardless of their sexual orientation or identity. As supervisor, you can set the tone for your department or unit by your responses to LGBTQ issues. Respond to negative remarks or jokes in a way that demonstrates that you, and the library, do not tolerate this sort of disrespectful behavior. Other staff will respond similarly to the way you handle these situations. Educate yourself about LGBTQ issues if you are not already familiar with them. Learn more about local resources on campus or in your community; many campuses have LGBTQ offices that can provide information and assistance.

Physical Disabilities

In your role as supervisor, you are responsible for working with your library or organization to provide a welcoming and inclusive environment for all staff, including those with physical disabilities. Look for areas where your library or organization can improve access for individuals with physical disabilities.

For staff who are deaf or hearing impaired, always face the staff member when speaking with him or her. This will help the staff member to hear as much as possible and allow him or her to see lip-reading cues. Consider carefully the seating arrangement in the work area and at meetings. During meetings and presentations, be sure that seating is available to allow the staff member to hear as much as possible. When feasible, tape-record meetings so that the staff member can review them as needed.

For visually impaired staff, be sure that written documentation is clear, black-on-white copy. Policies and procedures should be conveyed verbally to the employee as well as in documentation accessible to the employee.

If mobility is an issue for a staff member, work with the employee to determine appropriate tools and work space configuration. If arm or hand mobility is limited, consider structuring job duties so that the staff member works together with another staff member for tasks that require lifting and so on. When speaking with a staff member in a wheelchair, sit down during your discussion so that you are both at the same eye level. Do not make assumptions about wheelchair users; lower body mobility may be their only difficulty. In this case, they are no different from any other staff person who is seated.

Importance of Recognizing Strengths

Recognizing the strengths of your individual staff members can help you to channel their activities in the way that will be most beneficial to your unit. A number of personality indicators or personality trait surveys can help individuals determine their areas of strength. As with all surveys or testing measures, their findings should be considered as just a small part of the package that individuals bring to their positions and should never be used to stereotype employees. As Gordon Lawrence states, "We tend to stereotype those who are most different from ourselves because we understand them less well—a rule that holds true for type differences as well as cultural, racial, etc."[11] As a supervisor, it is your responsibility to ensure that if your organization does use personality-type tests, you work with staff members in your unit to examine their own stereotypes and not impose them on their coworkers.

One common workplace personality assessment tool is Gallup's Clifton StrengthsFinder. The Gallup organization, over the course of many years of surveys and research, determined that the best managers have two assumptions about their staff: each person's talents are enduring and unique, and each person's greatest room for growth is in the areas of his or her greatest strengths.[12]

The following thirty-four patterns, or themes, are the most prevalent themes of human talent and the basis for the StrengthsFinder, introduced in the book *Now, Discover Your Strengths*, by Marcus Buckingham and Donald O. Clifton:

Achiever	Developer	Learner
Activator	Discipline	Maximizer
Adaptability	Empathy	Positivity
Analytical	Fairness	Relator
Arranger	Focus	Responsibility
Belief	Futuristic	Restorative
Command	Harmony	Self-Assurance
Communication	Ideation	Significance
Competition	Inclusiveness	Strategic
Connectedness	Individualization	Woo[13]
Context	Input	
Deliberative	Intellection	

The StrengthsFinder's purpose is to help individuals find the areas where they show the greatest potential for strength. For supervisors, recognizing areas of staff talent will enable them to help individual staff members make the most of their potential, the theme of "Individualization."[14] By focusing on each employee's individual strengths, you can adapt the way you work with the employee in areas such as your communication style, how you provide feedback, and how you motivate for optimal performance.[15]

Buckingham and Clifton provide suggestions for how to manage each of the themes or strengths of staff in *Now, Discover Your Strengths*.[16] Once you know the top themes for an employee, you can work together with the employee to develop his or her strengths.

Retention

Retaining a diverse workforce is crucial. Building a culture that is inclusive and welcomes diverse opinions and experiences is the first step in retention. There are many ways to change an organization's culture. Chapter 14 covered ways to assess organizational culture. One way that some libraries have adopted to build an inclusive culture is to become a learning organization. Learning organizations value sharing ideas throughout the organization. Members share experiences, skills, and expertise, and in doing so, they build respect for all members of the organization and create an organizational culture and work environment of inclusiveness. This provides a strong foundation for retaining a diverse workforce.

Important aspects of retention include on-the-job training, opportunities for challenging work, opportunities for advancement, flexible scheduling, competitive compensation, and other monetary and nonmonetary rewards. With an increasingly diverse and changing workforce, supervisors face new challenges. Issues related to single-parent households, dual-career parents, sandwich employees (i.e., those who are caring for their children as well as their own elderly parents), older workers, LGBTQ employees, and individuals with commitments outside of work and family life are increasingly common situations for human resources offices, employees, and supervisors.[17] Many libraries have made a commitment to providing staff with ongoing opportunities to develop the skills to function effectively in a diverse workplace. Check to see about training opportunities at your library or larger organization.

Summary

Today, diversity is much more than affirmative action programs and mandatory training. Affirmative action, while providing a framework to ensure fairness in hiring, has limited influence regarding long-term organizational change. Successful supervisors in diverse organizations possess attributes and skills that were not necessarily of great importance in more traditional organizations. These attributes and skills, sometimes described as core competencies or key behaviors, will enable supervisors to effectively manage staff and to move units and departments forward. Continuing to operate as usual, without taking advantage of the opportunities that a diverse workforce offers, will result in a unit falling behind institutional initiatives.

As a supervisor, you must be prepared to work with a varied and diverse staff. You should be aware of your own opinions or biases and how they might influence your interactions with staff who have different values. Flexibility and creativity will be key in this regard. When you treat people as individuals with their own strengths and you value each person's strengths, you will be well on your way to creating a climate that encourages and respects diversity. Figure 15.1 gives some helpful advice for supervising a diverse workforce.

FIGURE 15.1
Diversity Dos and Don'ts and Other Advice

Dos

- Be sensitive to differences among people.
- Treat everyone with interest, compassion, and sincere concern.
- Encourage everyone to participate (be supportive, especially if they are shy).
- Solve tough problems privately.
- Hold all staff accountable for diversity and inclusion issues.
- Admit we all have biases and learn to recognize and overcome your own.
- Be willing to say, "If I show prejudices, let me know."
- Take all people seriously.
- If you are having a problem, don't ignore it; seek assistance. Ask colleagues or the equity office or equivalent for help.
- Become a culturally sensitive supervisor and also encourage others to be advocates.

Don'ts

- Don't use these differences to form or respond to stereotypes.
- Don't jump to conclusions based on stereotypes.

(cont.)

FIGURE 15.1 Diversity Dos and Don'ts and Other Advice (cont.)

Dont's (cont.)

- Don't (or allow others to) stereotype or make jokes about people of color.
- Don't (or allow others to) stereotype or make jokes about women.
- Don't treat staff from underrepresented groups differently.
- Don't express amazement when minority staff or women do well.
- Don't be confrontational in public.
- Don't expect all African Americans or members of any ethnic group to have a particular accent or the same accent.
- Don't use people-of-color or female examples just as extremes (i.e., always negatively).
- Don't single out underrepresented staff to answer race/ethnicity questions; the same goes for women.
- Don't use power to hide personal mistakes.

Other Advice

- Understand that differences do exist among people.
- Recognize that these differences do affect how individuals interact in the workplace.
- Be observant of interpersonal interactions.
- Cultivate the habit of noticing the details of these interactions.
- Be especially observant about how you interact with your unit or department.
- Watch details such as eye contact and your pattern of involving staff.
- Create a context where people have names and distinct identities.
- Talk privately to staff who are always silent.
- Be careful about giving differential attention.
- Be extremely careful about casual remarks (especially those made quickly or stressfully).
- Learn to recognize your own racist and sexist language.
- Avoid racist and sexist language, correct others who use it, and ask that you be corrected.
- Seek out colleagues from underrepresented groups in your field for assistance.
- Recognize privilege and power and the roles both play in the life experiences others bring to the workplace.

SOURCE: Adapted and revised from "Thoughts on Diversity by UNL Faculty," a University of Nebraska–Lincoln internal document for campus faculty.

NOTES

1. Janice R. W. Joplin and Catherine S. Daus, "Challenges of Leading a Diverse Workforce," *Academy of Management Executive* 11, no. 3 (1997), 32.

2. Josh Bersin, "Why Diversity and Inclusion Will Be a Top Priority for 2016," *Forbes*, December 6, 2015, https://www.forbes.com/sites/joshbersin/2015/12/06/why-diversity-and-inclusion-will-be-a-top-priority-for-2016.

3. Bob Rosner, *The Boss's Survival Guide* (New York: McGraw-Hill, 2001), 187.

4. Sandra L. Colby and Jennifer M. Ortman, *Projections of the Size and Composition of the U.S. Population: 2014–2060* (Current Population Reports, US Census Bureau, March 2015), https://www.census.gov/content/dam/Census/library/publictions/2015/demo/p25-1143.pdf.

5. Taylor Cox, *Creating the Multicultural Organization: A Strategy for Capturing the Power of Diversity* (San Francisco: Jossey-Bass, 2001); Scott Page, *The Difference: How the Power of Diversity Creates Better Groups, Firms, Schools, and Societies* (Princeton, NJ: Princeton University Press, 2008).

6. For more on privilege and librianship, see April Hathcock, "White Privilege—See Also Library of Congress," *At the Intersection* (blog about the intersection of libraries, law, feminism, and diversity), November 5, 2016, https://aprilhathcock.wordpress.com/2016/11/05/white-privilege-the-library-of-congress.

7. Pat Burke Guild and Stephan Garger, *Marching to Different Drummers*, 2nd ed. (Alexandria, VA: ASCD, 1998), chapter 3.

8. Deborah Tannen, *You Just Don't Understand: Women and Men in Conversation* (New York: Ballantine Books, 1990), 43–44.

9. Deborah Tannen, *You Just Don't Understand: Women and Men in Conversation*, Quill edition (New York: HarperCollins, 2007), 24–25.

10. Sally Helgesen, *The Female Advantage: Women's Ways of Leadership* (New York: Doubleday Books, 1990), 19–24.

11. Gordon Lawrence, *People Types and Tiger Stripes: Using Psychological Types to Help Students Discover Their Unique Potential*, 4th ed. (Gainesville, FL: Center for Applications of Psychological Type, 2009), 105.

12. Marcus Buckingham and Donald O. Clifton, *Now, Discover Your Strengths* (New York: Free Press, 2001), 8.

13. Ibid., 81.

14. Ibid., 171.

15. Ibid., 174.

16. Ibid.

17. Ellen Ernst Kossek and Sharon A. Lobel, eds., *Managing Diversity: Human Resource Strategies for Transforming the Workplace* (Cambridge, MA: Blackwell, 1996), 230.

Policies and the Legal Environment

Policies and procedures are the organization's way of defining roles and responsibilities. They set the boundaries for individual actions, defining how managers interact with the organization. Many organizational policies are developed to address legal issues and to outline how the organization implements various laws and regulations.

As a manager, you need to be aware of the legal responsibilities of your position and you need to know how your organization handles those legal issues. You will also want to know what assistance you can expect from the organization if you do have a problem and what liabilities you face as a manager. As a manager, you are legally responsible for responding to problem situations. Not acting on personnel issues, for example, can be as dangerous for you individually as taking the wrong action would be. For example, if you are aware of a case of alleged sexual harassment in your organization, even if it is not in your unit, and you do not report it, you could still be liable. Once you, as a manager, are aware of a problem, the organization is assumed to be aware of the problem. Failure to act can result in the employee winning a complaint or suit against the organization because you neglected to act.

Rather than running from your role as manager in order to avoid legal entanglements, you can significantly decrease the chances of situations going awry by following good personnel management practices. You can protect yourself as a supervisor when you create a collaborative working environment instead of a litigious environment.

US Employment Laws

Employment laws are numerous and complex because there are various federal laws, state laws, executive orders, and local laws and regulations regarding the selection of employees and the treatment of individuals in the workplace.[1] Some laws apply only when an organization reaches a certain number of employees, while others apply to all organizations. The laws and regulations in the employment area change as new laws are passed, as courts render decisions, and as regulations are rewritten. It is your responsibility to remain current on changes in employment laws. Work with your organization's human resources and legal departments to stay abreast of changes that impact your organization. If your organization does not have the support systems you need, seek assistance from county or state offices; local, state, or national library associations; and other business and professional associations that can help you. Not knowing the law is not a valid excuse for acting inappropriately or not acting at all.

Many employment laws and regulations seek to protect employees from discrimination and harassment. Numerous laws and regulations define this important policy area as well as the concept of fairness in the workplace. Many of the policies that organizations follow relating to fairness started with the Civil Rights Act of 1964, which includes the concept of equal employment opportunity (EEO). The many guidelines surrounding EEO policies are meant to provide for equal opportunities for all without regard to race, religion, origin, or gender. Many organizations have also added sexual orientation to the list. EEO guidelines apply to hiring decisions, salary and compensation, promotion decisions, and firing decisions, as well as to how you manage the work within your unit. As a manager, you want to be sure that you are not discriminating against an individual because of that person's characteristics.

Another important law that you need to understand is the Fair Labor Standards Act (FLSA), passed in 1938, which outlines compensation issues, defines the forty-hour workweek, sets a minimum wage and overtime pay, and defines exempt and nonexempt employees. In 2014, President Barack Obama directed the Department of Labor to update the regulations defining which white-collar workers are protected by the FLSA's minimum wage and overtime standards and to modernize and simplify the regulations. In 2016, the Department of Labor published the final rule, which updated the overtime regulations with a focus primarily on salary and compensation levels needed for executive, administrative, and professional workers to be exempt. The final rule sets the standard salary, the total annual compensation requirement for highly paid workers subject to a minimum duties test, and establishes a mechanism for automatically updating the salary and compensation levels every three years.[2] Exempt employees are not covered by the requirements of the FLSA, while nonexempt employees are covered.

As a supervisor, be sure you are not asking nonexempt employees to work overtime unless they are compensated to do so. You will also want to be sure that employees correctly record time worked so that overtime is properly identified. It is not useful to have employees, for whatever reason, decide that they will simply work extra hours and not record the time. The organization is still responsible for ensuring that staff are appropriately paid. As the supervisor, you need to be sure that staff follow the rules so that the organization is not liable for violating the law.

The Equal Pay Act of 1963 also addresses the question of compensation and clarifies the concept of equal pay for equal work. This law prohibits an organization from paying women less than men for the same position and job tasks.

The Age Discrimination in Employment Act of 1967 makes it illegal for an organization to discriminate against people who are forty or older. As the workforce in libraries ages, and as staff postpone retirement, accusations of discrimination based on age could increase. Be sure you are not inadvertently discounting the contributions of older employees, stereotyping your staff, or withholding advancement opportunities from staff as they age.

The Occupational Safety and Health Act of 1970 sets standards for creating a safe and healthy working environment. As a supervisor, you have responsibilities for providing a safe working environment. This includes such issues as "ergonomic furniture, air quality and ventilation, placement of office machinery (photocopiers, printers, etc.), cabling."[3] While some of these issues may be handled by a central unit in the library, in your supervisory role, you are responsible for reviewing your own area for safety issues. Providing appropriate step stools, for example, for staff who shelve materials or need to reach materials from higher shelves is an example of providing a safe environment. Reminding staff not to stand on chairs to reach things is another example.

The Americans with Disabilities Act, passed in 1990, protects staff with disabilities from discrimination. The definition of *disability* is fairly broad and covers a wide range of conditions. The act also established the concept of "reasonable accommodations" for individuals with disabilities. Employers are required to make reasonable accommodations for a "disabled" person who is qualified for the position, unless doing so causes undue hardship to the employer's business. The person does have to be able to perform the essential functions of the position. Therefore, it is very important that the job description for the position incorporates all of those essential functions. Be sure to work with human resource staff to ensure you are following your organization's policies and practices related to ADA and accommodations.

Another important law is the Family and Medical Leave Act (FMLA). Passed in 1993, FMLA provides for job-protected leave for family or medical reasons as defined in the act. The reasons for using family and medical leave (FML) include a serious health condition that makes an employee unable to perform his or her job duties; the need to care for a spouse, child, or parent who has a serious health condition; and the need to care for a child after birth, adoption, or foster care. In 2009, regulatory changes for the FMLA added benefits to military personnel and refined the definition of the term *employer*. Check with your organization to find out when FML may be used and how the organization outlines the reasons for using FML as regulations in this area change. At a maximum, a person's position is protected for up to twelve weeks of FML per rolling calendar year. Leave may be with or without pay, depending on the organization's leave policies. Organizations need to have policies on how they implement FML, and you will want to be sure you understand how the law is handled in your organization.

You should carefully monitor changes in the laws in your state, county, or city that could impact your work as a supervisor. Some states have now passed anti–affirmative action laws that make it illegal for those in public institutions to discriminate against or grant preferential treatment to any person or group based on race, sex, ethnicity, or national origin.[4] Although you may hold any number of opinions about such laws, as a supervisor, your responsibility is to be aware of how this type of initiative impacts the way you make decisions. For example, in public institutions, these laws may impact hiring processes. While you may still seek a diverse pool of qualified candidates for a vacancy, you will want to have objective, defensible criteria for how the hiring decision is made. Again, it is important that as a supervisor you keep track of local changes that impact your legal environment.

These laws address some of the common issues you will face as a supervisor. They do not, however, cover everything you need to know as a manager. To find out more about which laws affect your work, consult with the human resources experts in your organization. Know when you should contact legal counsel for advice. Perhaps the best course of action as a manager is to remember that if you have any doubts about how to handle a personnel issue, ask for help rather than guess. Making a mistake or attempting to avoid a legal issue can be disastrous to you and the organization. Asking for help and getting legal advice can save you time and decreases the chances that problems will escalate.

Legal Issues Impacting Libraries

Personnel laws are not the only legal area that you need to monitor as a supervisor. In the library field, you should also be aware of and familiar with copyright laws, intellectual property laws, and electronic licensing issues. Of course, you should be knowledgeable about censorship issues, First Amendment rights, banned book issues, and equitable access to information, just to name a few areas that impact libraries. The ALA website provides information about the political and legal issues impacting libraries, and the Washington office of the ALA keeps track of legislation that may impact the field.[5] If you are a supervisor in a department with both librarians and staff, be sure that your staff, as well as the librarians, are aware of the key issues that impact the unit.

As a manager and supervisor work hard to create a positive working environment for your staff and practice good personnel management. When employees know the organization's policies regarding the many aspects of employment law and your staff recognize that you consistently follow those policies, you will be in good stead. Employees become concerned when they feel they are not being treated fairly. The challenge for you as a supervisor is to figure out what defines fair treatment within your unit and in your organization.

What Is Fair?

Definitions of the word *fair* include terms such as *reasonable*, *unbiased*, *done properly*, and *free from self-interest or prejudice*. Notice that being fair is not treating everyone the same, nor is it treating everyone equally. Rather, fairness means treating people as individuals while following standards and policies. Fairness means that everyone has the opportunity to compete for positions, for rewards, and for advancement. It does not mean that everyone will advance. Staff will have the opportunity to apply for or seek new challenges. It does not mean that everyone will succeed.

To create a unit where staff feel they are treated fairly, the rules and guidelines for how decisions are made, how staff are evaluated, and how promotions are granted need to be clear and understandable. When staff understand the rules, they are more likely to understand how decisions are made and why they may or may not get a promotion or other rewards.

When guidelines are clear, it is easier to show that personnel decisions are made as objectively as possible. For example, if you are responsible for recommending merit salary increases, then staff should understand what factors are taken into account when making salary decisions. If the performance evaluation is the basis for increases, then it will be important to demonstrate how the evaluation scores translate into dollars or percentage increases. If you cannot explain how you made your recommendation on merit increases, then you will be creating an environment that will foster suspicion. You will not be seen as fair by your staff.

Discrimination

A perceived lack of fairness can result in accusations of discrimination or harassment. Discrimination and harassment are complex areas that you need to understand as a manager. You need to know your own biases and be sure you are not making decisions or taking actions based on them. While you may not be able to eliminate your own biases, you can understand them and can refrain from using a prejudiced view in the workplace.

Besides understanding yourself, as a manager, you need to understand the complex legal perspective of discrimination and harassment. Again, know your organization's policies in this area. Be sure you are clear on how to recognize and respond to inappropriate behavior in the workplace. Failure to act on cases of discrimination or harassment could make you as liable as the person who is exhibiting the inappropriate behavior.[6]

To help create an environment where it is clear that discrimination and harassment will not be tolerated, you can do the following:

Act when you hear about behavior that makes you suspicious.

Talk to employees who may be involved in inappropriate actions or find out what has occurred.

Remind staff about organizational policies on workplace behavior.

Take appropriate action based on organizational policies and procedures.

Encourage staff to report incidents of inappropriate behavior. Help staff understand that reporting problems is not "tattling" on fellow workers but is protecting all members of the unit and organization from potential problems.

Investigate or report complaints that come to you, following organizational policies and procedures. Do not dismiss a complaint because you cannot imagine the staff member behaving inappropriately.

Do not tolerate inappropriate jokes and stories. Nothing in the workplace is "just kidding."[7]

Most important, document your actions. You will need the written evidence as you pursue an investigation, and if the organization is going to be able to take action, you will need to show that the problem was handled appropriately.

Accusations of discrimination or harassment must be addressed. You can be successful when you carefully follow your organization's policies, consult with the proper authorities, document what you have done, and take time to carefully address the problem. These problems will not go away. You must address them in order to resolve them and to again create or re-create a positive working environment.

Handling Complaints

Despite your best efforts to demonstrate fairness, staff members may still feel that they are not receiving the same benefits as others in the unit. Complaints may arise when someone in the unit receives a promotion, a larger raise, or additional training opportunities. When you are faced with a staff member questioning your actions, you can handle the situation most effectively by taking time to listen carefully to the staff member and by being prepared to explain your decision. The steps you take will depend on how your organization handles any particular problem. However, in any situation, you need to actively address the issue. This is not the time to hide or to try to cover up a problem. The sooner the organization can address a problem, the more likely the issue will be successfully resolved.

What are some ways you can begin to address a concern? Imagine you are deciding whom to promote in your unit. You have two possible internal candidates, Sally and Jane. Based on qualifications, you choose Sally. However, Jane believes she should get the promotion because she has been in the unit longer. Jane accuses you of being unfair. What should you do? When faced with an accusation of unfairness regarding a promotion decision, try the following techniques.

Plan ahead for potential questions by having a clear set of criteria for personnel decisions. Make sure that job advertisements for promotion opportunities outline the skills needed for the position and the qualifications that are sought.

Prepare for a conversation with an unhappy staff member by reviewing your notes about how you made your decision. This is not the time to guess at what you did or to be vague about the process you used to make a decision.

Focus on the staff member who has questioned the decision and not on the person who received the promotion. Maintain confidential information and do not reveal personal information about the successful candidate. In other words, do not explain why the other person got the promotion. Instead, explain what skills were needed and review the qualifications as noted in the announcement of the position. Then review the staff member's performance regarding those skills. This approach assumes you have documented any skill or performance issues in the annual performance review. This way you can refer to written documentation that the employee has already seen to illustrate your points about skills.

Be direct and factual, yet sensitive to your employee's feelings. Treat the staff member with respect.

Focus on the staff member's strengths and how he or she can improve his or her performance and develop the skills needed for other promotional opportunities. However, be very careful that you do not promise that the person will succeed the next time he or she applies for a promotion.

Discuss development plans and career goals with the staff member. Turn the conversation into an opportunity to help with career planning.

Do not expect the staff member to agree with your decision or to thank you for the conversation. Instead, give him or her time to reflect on the conversation.

Follow up later with the staff member about ideas for career development. Help the staff member find ways to use his or her strengths to excel and thereby possibly qualify for rewards and advancement opportunities.

Fairness is all about helping staff to become the best employees they can become. If you are consistent in how you apply policies and rules and are clear about your expectations for workplace behavior, you will be successful at creating an environment that helps staff feel they are respected and are being treated fairly.

Why Problems Develop

Problems can develop in an organization when the top management and the organization do not take time to generate and implement appropriate personnel policies and procedures. But procedures alone will not resolve problems. Once policies and procedures are in place, management must ensure that everyone does the following:

> *Receives appropriate training.* Inadequate training of supervisors increases the chances that supervisors will not respond appropriately to problems.
>
> *Follows written agreements.* Not adhering to written contracts and union agreements will result in problems for the manager and the organization.

> *Consistently enforces procedures.* Policies and procedures apply to all members of the unit. Excusing poor performance by one person while expecting compliance by others will result in problems.
>
> *Clearly understands fair treatment.* Perceived unfairness will cause staff unrest and create problems for the unit and the manager.[8]

As a supervisor, take time to learn about employment laws, policies, and regulations. Then follow the policies in a consistent manner. You will be more successful as a supervisor when you are perceived to be fair.

Summary

As a manager, you are responsible for knowing and following the organization's policies, particularly those based on employment laws. Employment laws change as current cases are decided, regulations are written, or legislative action occurs. Be sure you keep informed about changes that impact your workplace. Ignorance of the law is not an excuse for inappropriate actions. When in doubt, seek advice from your personnel office or legal counsel.

Your best defense as a supervisor is to be fair and consistent. Creating a good working environment where staff are productive and feel respected will go a long way toward eliminating potential legal problems.

NOTES

1. Gary McClain and Deborah S. Romaine, *The Everything Managing People Book* (Avon, MA: Adams Media, 2002), 204.
2. US Department of Labor, Wage and Hour Division (WHD), "Final Rule: Overtime," accessed October 16, 2016, www.dol.gov/whd/overtime/final2016.
3. Bob Pymm and Damon Hickey, *Learn Library Management*, 2nd ed. (Friendswood, TX: Total Recall, 2007), 80.
4. Valerie Richardson, "Obama Helped Defeat Anti-Affirmative Action," *Washington Times*, November 8, 2008, www.washingtontimes.com/news/2008/nov/08/obama-helped-defeat-anti-affirmative-action.
5. See American Library Association, "Office of Government Regulations," ALA.org, accessed February 21, 2017, www.ala.org/advocacy/advleg/federallegislation.
6. McClain and Romaine, *Everything Managing People Book*, 211.
7. Ibid., 212.
8. Deryl Leaming, *Academic Leadership* (Boston: Anker, 1998), 111–12.

Career Management

While you are busy supporting the development of your staff and helping them plan and advance their careers, don't forget about yours. It is important to take time to plan your own career. Take a moment to think about where you are in your career and where you want to be. Even if you already have a career plan, changes in the field, in your organization, and in your life can impact your career plans and how you feel about your career.

Career management has changed over the years. In the twentieth century, a career implied working for one organization, and that's what many people did. Employees spent thirty or more years with the same organization or system and did not consider changing jobs. Today, we live in a world where some of our staff will have several careers and may move among fields. Changing jobs every couple of years is becoming more common. Employees look for ways to stay engaged, refreshed, and challenged. If their current jobs do not keep them challenged and enthusiastic, they look for opportunities at other libraries. The same may be true for you. If so, you can take steps to keep your career moving forward.

Stages of Career Development

Traditionally, careers proceeded through the following stages: exploration, organizational entry, establishment, maintenance, and finally disengagement.[1] You started by learning about a career area, usually through higher education options. Perhaps you worked in a library as a student. You found out more about the field and the job options for librarians and information scientists and pursued education in this area.

Next, you searched for a position in your area of interest. The library and information science field has broadened in the past fifteen years, with new opportunities in libraries and in other related industries. Finding a satisfying first job can be a real challenge. Once on the job, you need to build the skills that will make you a valuable employee.

As time goes on, you learn your position and maybe take on some new responsibilities. Before you know it, you reach a midcareer level. This is a good time to assess where you are in your career. Are you satisfied with the skills you have? Do you enjoy what you do? If not, it's time to make changes. If you are satisfied with your career, then be sure to examine how you can keep your skills current and continue to grow in our rapidly changing information environment.

The final stage of a career is retirement or disengagement. Today, that might happen at age fifty-five or seventy, as some employees retire early and others stay in the workforce beyond the traditional retirement age. At this point, you look at what new things you want to do and how you will change your life for either retirement or a new career.

While these are the traditional steps in career development, people entering the workforce now may have three, four, or more careers. Their planning time frame will be shorter, but they will still experience these five stages of career development.

Nontraditional Careers

As career paths have changed, the linear path described in the previous section is less common and may not relate to your experience or be the type of path you would like to pursue. Recognize that there are various career paths you might take. The ALA website offers options for nontraditional roles in libraries and other businesses and organizations.[2] Some vendors and publishers employ librarians to help design products and services and also as sales representatives. Other career paths might include positions in human resources, public relations or marketing, database administration, and Web design and user experience or as chief information officers (CIOs) in businesses and higher education, information architects, and usability researchers.

Plateaus

Career plateaus can occur even when you have carefully planned your approach to career development. Structural plateaus occur when there are no promotional opportunities left in your current organization. Here, your option for upward mobility is limited to finding positions in other organizations.[3]

Content plateaus occur when you have mastered the tasks of your position and find you have no more challenges. Content plateaus are less likely to occur in the information field, where changes in technology and in information resources add interest and change to our positions. Opportunities for learning abound in our field, and you should take advantage of learning opportunities that your library or larger organization may provide.

Plateauing can also occur when we feel we can no longer advance and see this lack of change as a failure in our lives. Staff who measure their self-worth by their jobs can be vulnerable to such feelings. As a manager, you will want to be sure you do not become so focused on your job that you neglect other areas of your life.

Personal Guidance

To manage your career, you should decide where you want to go and then design strategies to get there. You may want to carry out your own strategic planning process for your career.

Begin with a vision, just as you do for your organization or unit. Describe what kinds of positions you want. Where do you want to be in five or ten years? What aspects of the information field are most exciting to you? What jobs do you see around you that look interesting and exciting?

Decide, too, what kinds of organizations you want to work in. Do you prefer small organizations, multibranch systems, large organizations, or commercial, nonprofit, or public institutions? Thinking through the characteristics of an organization that are important to you will help you as you map out your career.

Next, it is time to do your own SWOT analysis of your strengths, weaknesses, opportunities, and threats. Look at what skills you have and which ones you need to develop. Think about the options you have to build your career and the barriers that can slow your progress.

Use this information to help focus your planning so you can capitalize on opportunities as they arrive. Look for projects that will help you gain experience and round out your skill set. Add to and refine your options as you assess changes that can impact your own goals.

Stay flexible. The information field is always changing. Jobs change and organizations change. You may miss opportunities to advance if you stick too closely to your plan.

Keep Up with the Field

Pay attention to how the field is developing.[4] Read publications from professional associations and trade magazines. Join ALA and other pertinent associations in the field and attend conferences and meetings. Join association committees that match your interests.

Trends. Keep up with the literature about the information field. Read what trends, changes, and new options are developing. By staying aware of how the field is changing, you can assess how you can use these changes to your advantage.

Technology. Keep current on technology. As our library users move from computers to laptops to tablets to smartphones to wearable devices for their information, we need to move with them. Be aware of these changes. By keeping your skills current, you will stay more employable and better able to control your own career options.

Networking. You also want to be sure you continue to network with colleagues, managers, vendors, and others even as you move through management positions. Your personal network can help you assess your career options as well as help alert you to changes that may be harmful to your own advancement. LinkedIn is one social media source for networking.

Mergers and reorganizations. Finally, be aware that mergers and reorganizations can occur and can change the direction your career is taking. Library systems can merge, and certain types of libraries are now merging or downsizing. Schools and corporations may be eliminating their libraries. There are fewer vendors each year as firms merge. While you cannot anticipate every possible change, you can stay prepared for changes by watching for signs of economic problems and by watching how top decision makers are assessing the organization. As you learn to read between the lines in announcements of changes, you can prepare yourself for them. By keeping your skills up-to-date and your options open, you will have a better chance of thriving in an economic downturn or major restructuring effort.

Personal Balance

While you are working on your career plans, you should also consider how to manage your personal life. You are a whole person, not just a library leader. Personal wellness, family health, and work effectiveness are all related. You are more effective at work when you take care of your own well-being and develop a positive life outside of your job.[5]

You can apply the same planning techniques you use to assess your career to planning your personal life. Begin by identifying your personal values. Decide what things are most important to you. Think about how you rank social interactions, friends, family, religious values, a home, time for recreation, and so on. Decide, too, how you like to spend your time. How much time do you want or need for work, sleep, social activities, home maintenance, and so on? Putting these two lists together will help you focus your time.

Set realistic goals for yourself, given the things you need to do and want to do. Use these goals to design your own personal action plan of how you will spend your time. Decide what is important to you and find ways to build in time for these activities. If leading your daughter's Girl Scout troop or coaching your child's soccer team is a high priority, then look at how to arrange your job so you have time for these activities. If you value volunteering, find ways to do so in your community in a way that works with your schedule.

And then leave yourself time for fun and relaxation. Try to remember that you cannot control every minute of your day. Do take time to relax and enjoy yourself. This time will help you stay refreshed and better able to balance your work and personal lives.

If you are having trouble doing planning by yourself, consider talking to someone in your human resources department at work for ideas. Your institution may have offices that assist with career planning. A life coach can help you set boundaries and create a balanced life. Some health clubs have courses to help you with life-planning issues. Look around your area and find resources that can help you as you plan your career and your life.

Managing Stress

No matter how well you take care of yourself, you will find yourself under pressure and will experience stress. There are two kinds of stress: eustress and distress. Eustress is beneficial stress that leaves us feeling positive. We can experience eustress when playing sports, watching a suspenseful movie, or tackling a new challenge at work. The term *eustress* comes from a combination of the Greek prefix *eu-*, which means good, and *stress*. Eustress is good stress. Distress, on the other hand, has negative implications. Distress is the type of stress discussed in the remainder of this section.

Too much distress can cause anxiety or depression. A key to surviving the pressures of everyday life is to learn to manage distress as best you can. There are numerous techniques or rules that can help you deal with this stress in a constructive manner.

Take a deep breath. Recognize that you will not always be right. Mistakes do happen. Other people have better ideas. Do your best and recognize that you are doing so. Accept that sometimes you will not be first, nor will you always be the best.

Do not let stresses build up. Handle little situations as they occur to prevent large problems. For example, do not wait until the last minute to start a project. Set up a timeline that lets you work on a project and allows for problems to arise and be handled before the deadline.

Learn what situations cause you stress and develop strategies for handling these situations. For example, if you know you become stressed if you are late for an appointment, then plan your day to try to arrive ten minutes early. If something comes up that delays you, you are still likely to be on time. By pausing to study your own reactions to different situations, you can learn to control your own reactions and behaviors. You can decrease your distress by decreasing the number of times you are surprised or caught off guard.

Both eustress and distress are natural parts of our lives. By learning to manage stress, you can decrease the effect stress has on your life, your health, and your work.

Summary

Remember to take time to take care of yourself and your career. Think carefully about how to plan your personal life and your work life. As a busy manager, you may scoff at the idea of work-life balance. Find the right formula or equation for yourself. Develop goals and plans that help you meet your needs as you work to ensure that your staff and unit meet the organization's needs. You will not be an effective leader if you neglect your own life, become frustrated, and get burned out. Instead, take time to reflect and plan so you can enjoy your life and your career.

NOTES

1. Patricia Buhlen, *Alpha Teach Yourself Management Skills in 24 Hours* (Indianapolis, IN: Alpha Books, 2001), 188.
2. See American Library Association, "Library Careers," ALA.org, accessed February 21, 2017, www.ala.org/educationcareers/libcareers; and American Library Association–Allied Professional Association, "Occupation Resources," ALA-APA.org, accessed February 21, 2017, http://ala-apa.org/occupation-resources.
3. Buhlen, *Alpha Teach Yourself Management Skills*, 190.
4. Gary McClain and Deborah S. Romaine, *The Everything Managing People Book* (Avon, MA: Adams Media, 2002), 261–81.
5. Edward Betof and Frederic Harwood, *Just Promoted! How to Survive and Thrive in Your First 12 Months as a Manager* (New York: McGraw-Hill, 1992), 233.

Index